Rickenbacker
ELECTRIC **12** STRING

Rickenbacker
ELECTRIC 12 STRING

THE STORY OF THE GUITARS, THE MUSIC, AND THE GREAT PLAYERS
TONY BACON

Rickenbacker Electric 12-String

THE STORY OF THE GUITARS, THE MUSIC, AND THE GREAT PLAYERS

by TONY BACON

A BACKBEAT BOOK
First edition 2010
Published by Backbeat Books
An Imprint of Hal Leonard Corporation
7777 West Bluemound Road,
Milwaukee, WI 53213
www.backbeatbooks.com

Devised and produced for Backbeat Books by
Outline Press Ltd
2A Union Court, 20-22 Union Road,
London SW4 6JP, England
www.jawbonepress.com

ISBN: 978-0-87930-988-6

DESIGN: Paul Cooper Design
EDITOR: Siobhan Pascoe
PHOTOGRAPHY: Nigel Bradley, Miki Slingsby

Origination and print by Wai Man Book Binding (China) Ltd

10 11 12 13 14   5 4 3 2 1

CONTENTS

THE ELECTRIC 12-STRING STORY 6–126

A complete history from Rickenbacker's earliest days in the 30s, through competing instruments by Fender, Gibson, Danelectro, and others, to current instruments and players, plus an accompanying gallery of full-colour pictures.

MODEL DIRECTORY 127–155

Every Rickenbacker model, 12-string and 6-string, spec'd and explained, from 1932 to 2009, in this unique reference section. Plus systems for dating, including serial number keys, and a comprehensive timeline of models.

George Harrison can't wait, so he climbs wearily out of bed and peers into the guitar case on the floor. The instrument inside is amazing. He's never seen anything like it before, and he glances around the hotel room to see if his bandmates agree. They're grinning. George is unwell – but this guitar is enough to make anyone feel better. It's big and red and inviting. It's an electric 12-string, and the guy that brought it says it's only the second one Rickenbacker has made. And now, all of a sudden, it's his.

The Beatles have been in the United States just a couple of days. It's the first week of February 1964 and it's their first time in America, where they'll play a few concerts and appear on Ed Sullivan's TV show. Already the group are causing pandemonium in New York City. Rushed from press conference to hotel to television studio and back again, the four British musicians are at the epicentre of a Beatlequake. But more important than any of that, Harrison has his hands on an actual American guitar.

George Harrison bought his first real American guitar, a Gretsch Duo Jet, through a newspaper ad back in Liverpool, three years earlier, in 1961. Later he got a couple more Gretsches. "Any good American guitar looked sensational to us," he said. "We'd only had beat-up crummy guitars at that stage."[1] John Lennon was the first Beatle to own an American guitar: he bought a Rickenbacker 325 in Hamburg in 1960 (of which more later).

Harrison had never had a 12-string before, electric or acoustic. He certainly knew about acoustic 12-string guitars, the kind that the sensitive folkie strummers used. He'd been enthralled when in 1963 he played a Stan Francis acoustic owned by Tom Springfield of The Springfields. Harrison recalled: "He had a big 12-string guitar, which he'd had made for him – in Liverpool, strangely enough. I asked if I could have a go, and borrowed it, and sat in the dressing room all the afternoon playing it. What a sound on it!"[2]

But what a sound on this new guitar. And an electric 12-string was something new for him – the same went for most other guitarists, too. It was also new to Rickenbacker, the California-based firm who'd made the thing. Rickenbacker's boss, F.C. Hall, had come over specially to the East Coast to show The Beatles some of his new gear, including the prototype 12-string.

It was an inspired move that would earn Rickenbacker untold sales during the 60s and well beyond. As a result of Hall's foresight, Harrison ended up with a fabulous gift of this new 12-string electric. John Lennon also benefitted when Hall arranged to provide him with a gleaming new-look version of the Beatle's Rickenbacker 325 model. It would arrive the following week in time for the group's second *Ed Sullivan* appearance.

Harrison waited until he was back in England to use his new toy properly. You can still hear the studio debut of his chiming 12-string (and Lennon's soloing 325) on the exuberant 'You Can't Do That', recorded on February 25 1964 – Harrison's 21st birthday.

He continued to use his 12-string all over the group's studio work and for some live performances. At the time, he compared the Rick 12 sound to that of an organ or an electric piano – which makes perfect sense when you hear some of the sounds Harrison gets from it on the *Hard Day's Night* LP. Perhaps the guitar's most famous studio moment is on the opening chord of the title song, 'A Hard Day's Night'. Countless musicians, famous and unknown, heard him on the record and saw him in the movie – and they all wanted a Rickenbacker 12.

"That sound," Harrison said much later, "you just associate with those early 60s Beatle records. The Rickenbacker 12-string sound is a sound on its own."[3]

What was it that made Rickenbacker produce an electric 12-string guitar? There were few precedents for such a guitar, and the temptation now is to see it as a lucky fluke. But to understand what was happening at Rickenbacker in the 60s, we need first to look into the company's beginnings and early years.

The story of Rickenbacker guitars goes back beyond the start of the 20th century and to a man named Adolph Rickenbacker. He was born in Basel, Switzerland, in April 1887, but just a few years later his family moved to the United States, at first living in Ohio and later Illinois. Eddie Rickenbacker, a cousin of Adolph's born in Columbus, Ohio, became a fighter pilot in the US 94th Pursuit Squadron during the 1914–18 World War. Eddie shot down 27 German aircraft, earning him the coveted title "ace of aces".

In 1918, Adolph finally moved to Los Angeles, California, and two years later established a successful tool-and-die firm, stamping out metal and plastic parts to customers' requirements. It's possible that Adolph may have offered these facilities to help cousin Eddie and his ill-fated attempt to manufacture Rickenbacker automobiles in the 20s. Generally, however, Adolph did very well from the tool-and-die work – and did even better when he married Charlotte Kammerer, a native of Pennsylvania who was rich through family connections in the oil business.

In the late 20s, work for guitar makers formed a profitable strand for the Rickenbacker Manufacturing Company. One especially enthusiastic customer for Adolph's metal parts was the National String Instrument Corporation, based close to Rickenbacker's premises in Los Angeles.

National started to specialise in the production of the ampliphonic resonator acoustic guitar. The novel idea was to suspend resonating aluminium cones inside a metal body as the structural basis for a series of loud, distinctive instruments. Adolph Rickenbacker had bought stock as a result of his business dealings with National – Rickenbacker's shop made metal bodies and resonator cones for National – and Adolph was nominally pictured as company engineer in National's publicity leaflets.

It was John Dopyera or George Beauchamp who invented National's resonator guitar – the stories provide conflicting evidence – and more likely a combination of the two. Dopyera was originally an instrument repairer who went on to join his brothers over the years to manufacture National guitars and also, later, Dobro guitars.

Beauchamp was a Texan vaudeville guitarist and a keen tinkerer. He lived in Los Angeles. Some years later, Adolph Rickenbacker wrote a short history about his early business activities, and in it he mentioned Beauchamp's departure from Texas. "His pappy gave him a mule and an old wagon and told him to 'git', and that is about all he had with the exception of an old guitar. Things were pretty tough those days for the guitar player, as the guitar was not loud enough to be heard in a band or orchestra. George got to using his head, as that was about the only thing he had left, besides his pretty wife."[4]

Like many performers in the 20s, Beauchamp was fascinated by the potential for making conventional flat-top and arch-top acoustic guitars louder. Musicians playing in ensembles demanded more volume than such guitars could reasonably offer, and apparent mechanical solutions began to appear such as National's loud resonator instruments.

Some stories suggest that Beauchamp originally approached John Dopyera with a request to attach a peculiar horn to a guitar in order to increase its volume. Dopyera complied – but from that transaction followed the rather more practical idea for a resonator. Author and musician Bob Brozman, who has documented the National story, describes George Beauchamp as "the catalyst for John Dopyera's radical ideas".[5]

Beauchamp became General Manager at National but apparently was still not content with the extra volume of the National guitars and their mechanical resonators. He started to wonder about the possibility of electric amplification – and once again he was not alone. Across the United States, and elsewhere too, players were experimenting with early, crude methods of amplifying their instruments. Some stuck record-player pickups into acoustic guitars and played them through the device's amplifier and loudspeaker, while others meddled with microphones.

Another potential solution was a purpose-built magnetic pickup for guitars, and this was what Beauchamp aimed at. As Adolph noted in his later account: "[George] had better ideas. If you can amplify radio waves, why not amplify vibration waves?"[6]

Beauchamp was helped by fellow National employee Paul Barth, a nephew of the Dopyeras, and started to put together a basic magnetic pickup system for guitars. Household gadgetry proved useful: Beauchamp used a washing-machine motor to wind the coils for the pickup. His son Nolan says: "My uncle had a Brunswick phonograph, and my father took the pickup out, extended the wires, and mounted it on a two-by-four [block of wood] with a single string. That's how he first proved that his theory was practical. He then began perfecting his six-string pickup."[7]

The theory of the electro-magnetic pickup is straightforward. Of course, as with most breakthroughs, it was Beauchamp's application of an apparently simple idea to a specific use that was inspired. A Rickenbacker leaflet of the 30s has a handy description: "Without going deeply into a technical detail, let us briefly explain how it works. A metal string vibrating before the poles of a magnet disturbs the field of magnetic force, and the sound waves are translated into electrical energy. These electric waves are then passed on to the [amplifier] enormously augmented and, by means of a speaker, delivered to the listener once more as sound waves. A rheostat provides perfect volume control. Sounds simple, doesn't it? Yet the inventor worked many weary months to perfect the device."

Beauchamp's experiments resulted in a pickup with a pair of horseshoe-shaped magnets enclosing the pickup coil and effectively surrounding the strings. When Beauchamp and Barth had a working version, probably around mid 1931, they roped in yet another National man, Harry Watson, to build a one-piece maple lap-steel guitar on which to mount the prototype pickup.

Nolan Beauchamp again: "Harry came over one day and made it by hand with a wood rasp, a hand coping saw, and a couple of clamps on an old beat-up bench in the back of our garage."[8] This was the wooden Frying Pan guitar, so-called because of its small round body and long neck. It is rightly famous today as the first guitar to feature an electro-magnetic pickup and in that sense is the basis for virtually all modern electric guitars.

Beauchamp, Barth, and Adolph Rickenbacker teamed up to put the ideas from this exciting prototype electric guitar into production. They formed the curiously named Ro-Pat-In company, together with a couple of other individuals, at the end of 1931 – just before Beauchamp and Barth were fired by National during a shake-up of that firm. The events could hardly have been coincidental.

In 1934, Beauchamp filed an application for a patent for what we now usually call the horseshoe pickup. The patent was eventually granted to him in August 1937 and had already been assigned to the company by an agreement dated December 1935. It was not unusual for patents to take this long to proceed through the system. Adolph said later that it took a demonstration for the patent officials to convince them of the pickup's viability. "The patent office wouldn't give us a patent because they didn't think it was feasible. So we sent I think it was [musicians] Danny Stewart, Dick McIntyre, and Sol Hoopii to Washington to play for about 15 minutes before the patent attorneys. It was only a few days before we got notice that our patent would be issued."[9]

In summer 1932, Ro-Pat-In started to manufacture cast aluminium production versions of the Frying Pan electric lap-steel guitar, each fitted with a horseshoe electro-magnetic pickup. We now recognise that these guitars are of great historical importance. While other makers such as Acousti-Lectric (later Vivi-Tone), National, Dobro, Stromberg-Voisinet (later Kay), Epiphone, and Gibson experimented during the 30s with electric guitars, Ro-Pat-In's Frying Pans were effectively the first electric guitars put into general production. Some of those better-known companies were producing mainly acoustic instruments, based on many years of experience. But the upstart Ro-Pat-In made only electric guitars.

Early examples of the Frying Pans usually had the Electro brandname on the heads, and as they were designed for the lap-steel or Hawaiian style of playing, where the player rests the guitar on his knees and slides a steel bar over the strings, players and collectors usually call them the Electro Hawaiian models.

By 1934, the Rickenbacker name – or to be more precise 'Rickenbacher' – had been added to the headstock logo. Adolph always used the original and, as far as he was concerned, correct un-anglicised version, spelt with an 'h' rather than a second 'k'. At first this was the way it appeared in the brochures and on the guitars with the new Electro

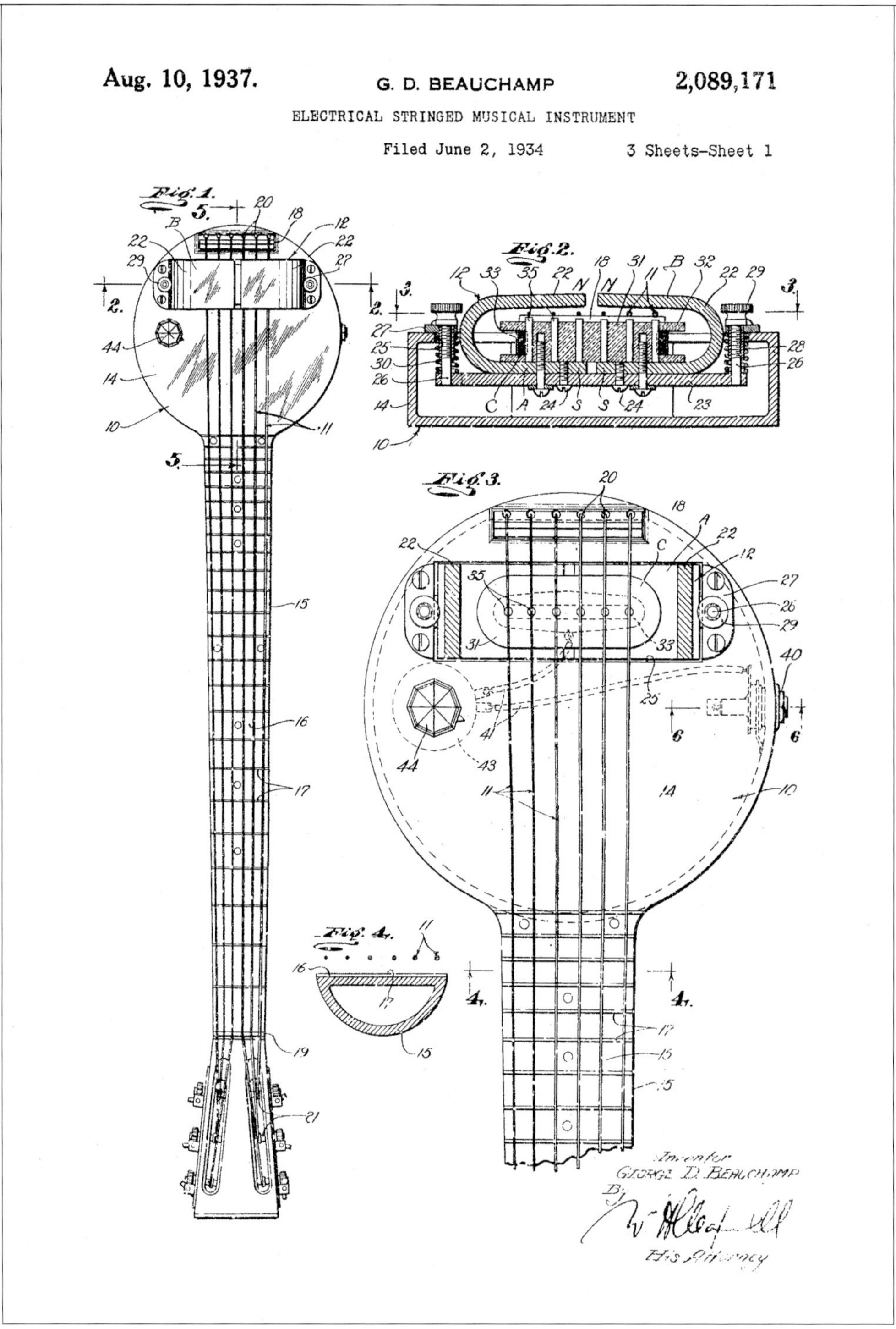

Aug. 10, 1937.   G. D. BEAUCHAMP   2,089,171

ELECTRICAL STRINGED MUSICAL INSTRUMENT

Filed June 2, 1934   3 Sheets—Sheet 1

Fig. 1.

Fig. 2.

Fig. 3.

Fig. 4.

Inventor
GEORGE D. BEAUCHAMP

By

His Attorney

● George Beauchamp invented the new "horseshoe" magnetic pickup (**patent**, left). Beauchamp was a partner in Ro-Pat-In, soon renamed the Electro String Instrument Company, along with **Adolph Rickenbacker** and **Paul Barth**. All three were pictured in a 30s brochure from **National** (below), another Los Angeles guitar-maker, with whom they had business links.

A. RICKENBACKER
ENGINEER

GEORGE D. BEAUCHAMP
SECRETARY-GEN. MANAGER

PAUL M. BARTH
VICE PRESIDENT

● At first, the name on the company's instruments was "Rickenbacher", with an h, as on the **30s logo** (right), revealing Adolph's Swiss roots. Later, the familiar spelling took over, with a k.

RICKENBACHER
ELECTRO
LOS ANGELES

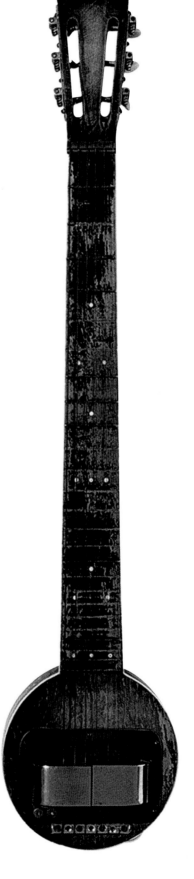

6 String $125.00
Complete with Speaker
7 String $135.00

The Seven-String Hawaiian Guitar
May also be had in the conventional six-string design.

● Adolph Rickenbacker (above) holds the 1931 electric lap-steel **Frying Pan**, shown right. This maple experiment was the world's first guitar to feature an electro-magnetic pickup, making it the basis for most electric guitars that followed. Adolph's Electro company made metal production versions, like the one (left) pictured in this 1932 Rickenbacker **catalogue**.

Rickenbacher brandname. Later, the familiar Rickenbacker spelling was adopted. A Rickenbacker family historian suggests that the change was made by some members of the family because they were nervous about misinterpretation of Germanic links during the World Wars. Also in 1934, the name of the manufacturing company was changed from Ro-Pat-In to the more logical Electro String Instrument Corporation.

Despite the innovative features, the early Electro and Electro Rickenbacher aluminium electric lap-steels did not sell in spectacular numbers. Electro probably sold little more than a dozen Hawaiian electrics in 1932, a poor record not helped by the depressed economy and the relative scarcity of electrical power in the country. Adolph wrote later: "The really difficult part was selling them and getting players to use them. Everywhere we would go they just would not have anything to do with the instrument. All the bands were afraid to use it in the fear that [an amplifier tube] would go in the middle of a number.

"We were finally allowed to demonstrate one on a stage show – that was our big moment! After setting it up and the player began to play, all at once the speaker of our amplifier announced 'KHJ Los Angeles' [a local radio-station broadcast]. The manager pulled the cord and practically threw us out! But George did not give up – he licked that trouble. But we still could not get anyone to play the electric guitar. After about two years of hard work and spending about $150,000, we were ready to give up."[10]

Around this time, Electro also produced some 'Spanish' wood-body electric guitars – in other words, guitars played in the way we now consider normal, as opposed to the lap-steels. The first, the Electro Spanish, appeared around 1932 – among the earliest of its kind – and the Ken Roberts model, named after an obscure local guitarist, followed about three years later.

These and other similar models consisted of conventional wooden acoustic guitar shells bought in by Electro from companies such as Harmony or Kay, two prolific guitar makers based over in Chicago. They were fitted with Electro's distinctive horseshoe pickup at the firm's Los Angeles workshop. "Think of the orchestral possibilities," suggested Electro's publicity. It seems that few players did. These wooden Spanish electrics, too, apparently sold in very small numbers.

Aluminium turned out to be an unsuitable material for the early Electro lap-steels. It expands in hot conditions – under stage lights, for example – and regularly conspired to put the guitar out of tune. Electro looked for a better material, and hit upon Bakelite. Later they also made lap-steels from stamped sheet metal.

Bakelite was the first synthetic plastic, a hard, tough, heatproof phenolic resin invented by the Belgian-American chemist Leo Baekeland in 1907 and popularised in the 30s for household objects. Adolph knew about Bakelite from his tool-and-die business, where he made plastic toothbrushes among other items. Electro produced guitars with the material after getting a licence from an Englishman, Arthur Primrose Young, who was granted a patent in 1932 that covered the production of moulded musical instrument necks and bodies.

The move to Bakelite was crucial to the story of Rickenbacker's electric Spanish guitars. In 1935, Electro produced its first guitars with the material, the Model B Hawaiian lap-steel and the Electro Spanish (later also called the Model B). They showed the usual differences between Hawaiian and Spanish versions: the Hawaiian featured a higher string action and typical 'square' cross-section of the neck; the neck joined the body at the 10th fret on the Hawaiian and the 14th on the Spanish.

The Bakelite Spanish was arguably the first 'solidbody' electric guitar. In fact, the small, waisted Bakelite body was semi-solid, but the tiny pockets under the thick, solid top were intended to reduce weight rather than add any acoustic resonance to the instrument.

"What would you say of a Hawaiian guitar you could hear a quarter of a mile away on a clear day, or a Spanish guitar louder than any piano?" queried an Electro leaflet of the 30s. "That's what we have in the new Rickenbacher Electro instruments." The Spanish Bakelite model didn't sell well, but the Hawaiian versions greatly improved Electro's position, in the United States and in export markets. The Hawaiians took off in the late 30s and are still regarded today as especially fine lap-steel guitars.

George Beauchamp ran the Electro guitar factory, based at South Western Avenue, Los Angeles, while Adolph Rickenbacker looked after the tool-and-die business in the other half of the building, so it seems that Beauchamp was again responsible for the introduction of the Bakelite models. However, after only a few years, Beauchamp apparently began to tire of the guitar business. In 1940, he sold his share interest and left Electro, reportedly to set up an operation to market fishing equipment, but he died shortly afterward. George Beauchamp, one of the great innovators of the modern electric guitar, was gone forever.

In his later account, Adolph summed up his feelings about the modest growth of Electro during the depressed 30s. "As I sit here writing this, I just happened to think – the doctor told me to get lots of rest and go to bed early. And as I go to sleep listening to some good Hawaiian music, I feel proud of George and myself that we did not let the guitar players down. And I don't know of any other thing that has ever happened to put so many boys back to work!"[11]

It was in the late 30s that Clayton Orr 'Doc' Kauffman came to the attention of Electro. Doc, originally from Kansas, played lap-steel guitar and violin, and was a relentless tinkerer. He became famous for a brief but important association with Leo Fender in the K&F company (K&F stood for Kauffman & Fender) in the 40s, before the Fender name was well known.

The first of Doc's inventions that Electro used was his vibrato unit, among the first hand-operated guitar-mounted devices for changing the pitch of strings and making vibrato effects. Kauffman reportedly came up with his Vibrola in the late 20s; his eventual patent is dated January 1932. The unit was crude and fragile. It worked with a sideways motion, in the same direction as the player's picking hand. To activate the unit, the player pulled the arm up, and a simple hinge let the tailpiece forward, flatting the pitch of the

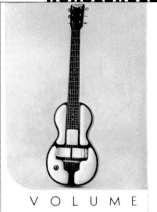

● The company's first electric hollowbody was this **Electro Spanish**, launched in 1932 and one of the first of its kind. They also made Bakelite semi-solid electrics, including the 1935 **Electro Spanish** (below centre, and right). **The Sweethearts Of The Air** (below) seen with a lap-steel Bakelite model (centre) and an Electro Spanish (right).

● The Rickenbacker Electro company made this **Ken Roberts model** (main guitar) from about 1935, named for a local musician who has since passed into obscurity. As with its other early hollowbody electrics, Electro bought in the neck and body, supplied for this model by Harmony of Chicago. Like the contemporary guitars on this page, it has a horseshoe pickup and a single volume control. The Roberts guitar also has a **Kauffman vibrato**, a crude pitch-wobbler invented by Doc Kauffman, whose **patent** for his "tremolo inducing" device is pictured opposite.

strings. When our player released the Vibrola's arm, a small spring returned the tailpiece (theoretically, at least) to its original position.

Electro made an exclusive licensing agreement with Doc in February 1936 to "manufacture, use, and vend the said invention for all fretted musical instruments" for an initial period of five years. Electro used it first on the Ken Roberts guitar and on various other Electro and Rickenbacker instruments until about 1960 – of which more later.

Rather more bizarre was Kauffman's patented motorised vibrato system, which the company built into its Vibrola Spanish guitar, or Vibratar, introduced at the end of 1936. Another of Electro's wonderfully over-the-top press announcements proclaimed the new model as "the most outstanding improvement in the Spanish guitar since the Moors brought the instrument from the Far East to Spain about the year 1088 AD".

The contraption was powered by an electric motor and fitted inside a modified Bakelite Electric Spanish model. A system of belt-driven arms and axles set a Vibrola in action, providing an automatic and constant vibrato effect that Doc hoped would emulate the sound of a violin. This additional metalwork resulted in a guitar even heavier than the standard Bakelite model, and it had to be supported by a stand.

Early takers included session guitarist Perry Botkin, whose employers included Al Jolson and Bing Crosby. He can be heard playing the instrument, unfortunately without vibrato, on the 1938 Brunswick recording of 'Hong Kong Blues' by Hoagy Carmichael. "No one seems to know just what is going on," Botkin wrote to Kauffman. "Several people have asked me about it since the record was released." Very few Vibrola Spanish models were sold. Electric guitars were unusual at the time, but this one was plain weird. Presumably Adolph's tool-and-die business was successful enough to finance the losses from these guitar projects.

Paul Barth, still with the company, received a patent for a version of the horseshoe pickup designed as a separate add-on item for acoustic guitars. It was also used on Electro's S-59 arch-top wood-body electric. After Beauchamp's departure from Electro in 1940, Barth did more and became factory manager after World War II. In summer 1942, Electro stopped making musical instruments and began production for the war effort. Adolph said later that they made vacuum control valves among other things.

During these years that the firm worked for the government, Adolph managed to extend the Los Angeles factory. Early in 1946, after World War II was over, the company got back to some sort of normal business. However, Adolph decided not to restore many of the musical instrument lines, including most of the poorly-received Spanish models. A lone exception was another wood-body electric, actually called the Spanish (or sometimes 'SP'). But Adolph seems to have lost interest in the electric Spanish guitar business. During 1946 he had turned 60, and it was probably around this time that he decided to sell the musical-instrument part of his operation.

To the rescue came Francis Cary Hall, generally known as F.C. Hall. He was born in Avon, Iowa, in September 1908, and moved with his family to California when he was around 11. In high school, he studied radio and electronics. This became his great interest and led to him owning only the second radio set in Orange County in south Los Angeles. His instructor had the first.

In his teens, Hall began a tentative money-making scheme by recharging the big batteries that radio sets required. Spotting a demand, he started a business to manufacture them by the late 20s. This developed into a radio repair store, Hall's Radio Service, and that led logically to a wholesale company that distributed electronic parts, the Radio & Television Equipment Co (often shortened to Radio-Tel). Hall set up Radio-Tel in Santa Ana, Orange County, in 1936.

One of Radio-Tel's customers was another Orange County-based radio repair store, Fender Radio Service, run by Leo Fender in Fullerton, some 15 miles from Santa Ana. Leo had set up the K&F company with Doc Kauffman, and the two started to make electric lap-steel guitars and small amplifiers toward the end of 1945. The following year, just after Leo and Doc ceased working together, Radio-Tel became exclusive distributors for the new Fender Electric Instrument Co, selling the company's electric lap-steels and amps with the new Fender brand.

By 1953, with the Telecaster electric solidbody guitar and the Precision electric bass also in production, Fender's business began to pick up. The existing sales arrangement with Radio-Tel was re-organised into the new Fender Sales company, based like Radio-Tel in Santa Ana and with four business partners: Leo Fender; F.C. Hall; Don Randall (general manager of Radio-Tel); and Charlie Hayes (a Radio-Tel salesman).

Later that year, F.C. Hall began to see the potential for running a musical instrument business where he not only distributed the product but also manufactured it. "I understood that Adolph Rickenbacker was interested in selling his instrument corporation," recalled Hall, "which I was told about through another person. Adolph's main interest was in the tool-and-die business, not the musical instruments."[12]

In late 1953, Hall bought the Electro String Music Corporation from Adolph. An agreement dated December 7 and signed by Adolph Rickenbacker (Electro president), Charlotte Rickenbacker (Electro assistant secretary), and F.C. Hall stated that the purchase was complete and that without any further payment Electro could continue indefinitely "to use the trade name 'Rickenbacker' in connection with the advertising and selling of all said electric guitars".

For a couple of years, Hall continued his association with Fender Sales. His experience working with Fender and his general view of the guitar business seems to have led him to consider that the way forward for Electro was to make electric Spanish-style guitars. The lap-steel business was still reasonably good, largely based on guitar schools, where students were encouraged to move on to better models as their skills improved. But in the early 50s, it appeared that the instrument's popularity had passed its peak, and so Hall began to set his sights on fresh targets for his new Rickenbacker business.

The guitar factory was still at South Western Avenue, Los Angeles. Hall recalled there

MODEL G—This instrument is a favorite with the professional players and non-professionals who desire an electric guitar that is distinctive and assures dependable performance. The professional styling of the Model G is enhanced by the polished gold chrome finish and gold-plated tailpiece and headcover plate.

Every one of the traditionally fine qualities of Rickenbacker instruments are to be found in this model. The control knobs and gold-backed fretboard are of clear lucite, and the fret and finger positions are white-filled and inversely carved to complete the pleasing design of the instrument. The instrument body is beautifully contoured and its construction is flawless.

Musicians throughout the country acclaim this Rickenbacker instrument as truly outstanding. It offers professional styling . . . pure tone quality . . . ease of playing . . . plus the "built-in" dependability of Rickenbacker electric guitars. Available with six or eight strings.

MODEL G

MODEL A-22

MODEL A-22 — This instrument retains the original body design of the first Rickenbacker electric guitar. Its time-approved polished aluminum body is durable and will retain its lustre for a long time. The single-unit pickup is chromeplated and position markings on the clear lucite fretboard are white-filled. Precision machined tuning keys will provide trouble-free use.

This model now has both volume and tone controls, conveniently located and spaced. Its design contributes to its being comfortable to play and easy portability. These features are combined with the finest electric guitar components to give the professional and non-professional musician an outstanding instrument that is a pleasure to own and play. The Model A-22 is available with six strings.

PERRY BOTKIN
Famed Radio Star—was one of the first to own an Electro Vibrola Spanish Guitar. Mr. Botkin supports such famous artists as Al Jolson, Eddie Cantor, Bing Crosby and others. Many other star guitarists, in most of the nation's top-flight broadcasts, use the Vibrola Spanish Guitar . . . Hugh Pendergraft, RKO Artist and Recordings; George Smith, Paramount Artist and Recordings; "Pinky" Tomlin, Composer and Radio Artist.

● Rickenbacker continued with metal-body guitars, as in this **50s catalogue** (above left), as well as wooden hollowbody electrics, like this late-40s **Spanish** or SP model (below). Hollywood session guitarist **Perry Botkin** (above) demos the 1937 **Vibrola Spanish**, with Doc Kauffman's built-in motorised vibrato system.

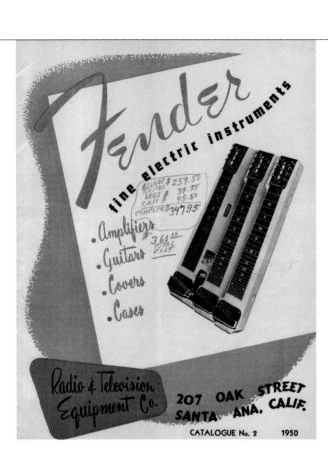

● **Francis Cary Hall**, pictured around 1958 (right), bought the Electro company from Adolph Rickenbacker. Hall was a businessman who began his career with a radio store. That led to his next venture, the Radio & Television Equipment Co, which distributed electronic parts. One of Radio-Tel's customers was Leo Fender, and in 1946 Hall's Radio-Tel operation became the main distributor of Fender's guitars and amps. The **1950 Fender catalogue** (above) notes Radio-Tel's HQ in Santa Ana. Hall, keen to make as well as distribute his own instruments, acquired Rickenbacker in 1953, and two years later his deal with Fender ended.

19

were about six employees when he bought it, including factory manager Paul Barth, and that they produced a small quantity of electric lap-steel guitars and amplifiers. Adolph Rickenbacker's tool-and-die business remained in the other half of the building. Radio-Tel's HQ had always been in Santa Ana, and in 1956 it moved from Oak Street to better premises at a new location on South Main Street.

Around the beginning of 1954, Paul Barth hired Roger Rossmeisl to work for Electro. Rossmeisl was born in 1927 near Kiel in the Schleswig Holstein region of northern Germany. His father, Wenzel Rossmeisl, was a keen jazz guitarist who started to build guitars around 1935. Wenzel used the brand Roger, named after his son. Following World War II, the Rossmeisls moved east to Berlin, opening a workshop there, and the teenage Roger began to learn about guitar-making. Shortly afterward, Wenzel established another workshop much further south while Roger remained in Berlin. Roger-brand electric models appeared by 1947; five years later, Roger Rossmeisl decided to emigrate to the United States.

Ted McCarty, president of the prestigious Gibson company in Michigan, received a letter from Rossmeisl asking if he could come to the United States and work for Gibson. "He was supposedly a master guitar maker, had a certificate from somebody in Germany," McCarty remembered somewhat disdainfully. "But anyway, I brought him over here. I paid his fare to come to work in our factory. He stayed about a year and left." McCarty said that Rossmeisl didn't get on too well with his fellow workers, some of whom were of Dutch descent and still disliked Germans so recently after the end of World War II, especially those like Rossmeisl with halting English.

"He wanted to make a guitar like a Gibson L-5," McCarty continued, "but *his* way, the way *we* should have. So we let him do it. I swear, the top was real thick, and clumsy … you could have used it as a bat." Maybe somewhere there exists a one-off Gibson Rossmeisl guitar? "Anyway," McCarty said, "after Rossmeisl left Gibson he went on vacation, and he got a job playing guitar on a ship going to Hawaii. Then he came back to Los Angeles. We never saw him again."[13]

Roger Rossmeisl joined Electro after his Hawaiian adventure, probably early in 1954, and it's likely that Paul Barth hired him specifically to work on new designs for Rickenbacker electric guitars. Evidently Rossmeisl's skills were improving rapidly.

That same year, the Electro company launched its first 'modern' electric guitars, the Rickenbacker Combo 600 (listed in the fall 1954 pricelist at $229.50) and Rickenbacker Combo 800 ($279.50). These first Combo models were aptly named, combining the horseshoe pickup and almost square neck of the earlier Hawaiian lap-steels with the up-and-coming solid-electric Spanish approach. Before he left Gibson, Rossmeisl must have seen the new Gibson Les Paul Model solidbody electric, launched in 1952, and there are some elements of that instrument in the Combo design.

It seems likely that Rossmeisl, Hall, and Barth shared the design work on the first Combo models. Hall said that he designed the control circuits and Rossmeisl was "one of the engineers involved", probably contributing the physical aspects of neck and body. Barth may well have been responsible for the mechanical components, such as the bridges, of the new guitars.

These first Combo models of 1954 shared an overall look: a carved-top body with two cutaways: the lower gently pointed; the upper more bulky. Some bodies were fully solid; others had the beginnings of a construction feature that, with later modifications, became typical of Rickenbacker. The back of the solid body was partly scooped out to reduce weight, and in these particular examples the back was then covered with a plate. Some necks were bolted on, others glued.

At first, the 600 and the 800 each had a single horseshoe pickup, although the 800 used one with double coils (the Rickenbacker catalogue of the time calls it a Multiple-unit). It was an early kind of humbucking pickup. Later versions of the 800 have two separate pickups: a horseshoe near the bridge and a more conventional-looking 'bar' type closer to the neck.

The first Combo models began to feature a brand new 'underlined' Rickenbacker logo on the headstock in the style still used by the company today. John Hall, the current owner of Rickenbacker, says that his mother, Lydia Catherine Hall (wife of F.C. Hall), designed the logo and the distinctive curved, pointed plate on which it appears. "She just got out her scissors and cut shapes out of paper and figured it out," he says. "It's a great logo, visible at 100 yards: there's no question as to what it is."[14] The typography is typical of the 50s, and the interlinked characters recall contemporary automobile logos designed as one continuous strip of chrome-plated metal.

The new Rickenbacker logo emphasised the fresh importance of this sole brandname for the company's guitars. F.C. Hall understood that solid-type Spanish electrics were the way forward. "I thought the new-style guitar would be more practical and would create more sales volume," he recalled. It didn't at first: the Combo guitars were slow sellers, and the guitars must have been a small part of Hall's Radio-Tel business at the time. He tried novelties. For example, some of these early Rickenbackers have a circular metal plate on the back of the body with a fitting for a saxophone-style carrying strap. This did not last.

Gradually, Rickenbacker became more adept at attracting musicians to its new designs. The company's next move was to abandon the clumsy horseshoe pickup and apply a more suitable unit to the Spanish electrics, like the designs used by other electric guitar makers of the time such as Gibson, Kay, Fender, Harmony, and Gretsch. The first model with the new pickup was the Combo 400, launched in 1956 (at $174.50). The 400 was also the first Rickenbacker with a new body shape, generally referred to now as the tulip style because of its outwardly curving cutaways. Another first was the through-neck, a feature that would become familiar on many Rickenbacker guitars.

As the name implies, a through-neck guitar has a neck that is not bolted or glued to the body – the usual methods – but one that extends through the length of the instrument, with 'wings' attached each side to complete the full body shape. A supposed

● The first "proper" six-string Rickenbacker electric after Francis Hall took over was the **Combo 800** (above), which was introduced in 1954. For now, Rickenbacker's old-style "horseshoe" pickup remained.

● When Francis Hall bought Rickenbacker in 1953, he wanted to develop a new line of guitars to compete with Fender. He hired German guitar-maker **Roger Rossmeisl** (seen with an experimental Rickenbacker acoustic, 1957, above). Rossmeisl devised the designs for which Rickenbacker is now famous, including the early models seen on these pages as well as the later hollow guitars. Hall was a keen photographer, and he snapped Rossmeisl (above) and the two women (left) who posed in 1956 with a blue Combo 600, bearing a horseshoe pickup, and a brown Combo 400 – this with the new type of pickup. Rickenbacker's archive will provide us with more examples of Hall's pictures in the coming pages.

● Appearing in 1956, the **Combo 400** (main guitar) was a slab-bodied, through-neck solid, priced below the carved-top Combo 600 and 800. It was the first Rickenbacker to feature a "tulip"-shape body and a more conventional pickup design.

benefit of this type of design is that the strings and their associated bridge, tailpiece, nut, and tuners are all located on the same piece of wood, enhancing sustain and tonal resonance. The through-neck design of Rickenbacker's Combo 400 of 1956 had few precedents, although one notable example was the historic Bigsby 'Travis' guitar, an early solidbody electric built by the California-based engineer Paul Bigsby in 1948 for his friend, the country musician Merle Travis.

Radio-Tel stressed the longevity of the Rickenbacker name in 1956 by promoting the 25th anniversary of the Frying Pan electric. "Twenty-five years ago the world first heard the music of the electric guitar," proclaimed an anniversary brochure. "It was the creation of the Electro String Instrument Corporation, manufacturers of Rickenbacker Electric Guitars. The introduction of this electronically amplified music launched a new era in the entertainment field."

F.C. Hall's relationship with the Fender Sales company ended in 1955. His position must have deteriorated as Rickenbacker's competing guitars hit the market. Charlie Hayes, one of the four partners of the Fender Sales company, was killed in a car accident in 1955, and there seems to have been disagreement among the other three about how to continue the partnership. "[Hall] bought the Rickenbacker company," explained one of them, Don Randall. "So we bought his interests in Fender Sales, which became Leo and myself."[15] Hall remembered: "When Charlie was killed, I decided that I would also turn in my stock. Randall and Fender handled the sale of it, settled on that basis."[16]

At least one of Radio-Tel's customers was unaware of this news. A dealer from Arizona tried to order Fender equipment from Radio-Tel in October 1957, and Hall wrote back politely informing him that Radio-Tel had not distributed Fender gear for some time. As a good businessman, Hall also took the opportunity to explain the virtues of Rickenbacker guitars, concentrating on the two-pickup Model 950, one of three new short-scale models that Rickenbacker had released that year. The other two new releases were single-pickup guitars, Model 900 and Model 1000.

At first the "three-quarter-scale" 900 and 950 appeared with a slightly revised version of the outwardly-curving tulip body, but later in the year Rickenbacker gave them a new shape with an inward-curving lower cutaway. Hall explained this in his letter to the Arizona dealer. "The guitar has the body cut in such a way that the 21st fret can be reached very easily, and chords can be played in the highest fret positions," he wrote. "This feature was added after the picture was taken for our catalogues, but all instruments which are now shipped will have this added feature." Rickenbacker offered the full-scale Combo 400 in the revised shape, and added the Combo 450 as a new model for 1957 as a two-pickup version of the 400.

Of much greater importance to Rickenbacker's long-term guitar designs was a pair of models launched in 1957, the Combo 650 and Combo 850. These guitars introduced a body shape that Rickenbacker has used in various incarnations and dimensions to the present day. The 650 and 850 were small-body guitars, and the elegant body style is distinguished by a sweeping crescent-shaped curve across the two cutaways. Rickenbacker referred to this new shape in a press release as the "new extreme cutaway body, permitting all frets on the slender neck to be reached with equal ease". The 650 and 850 were also among the first to contain Rickenbacker's new double-truss-rod system for correcting neck movement. In theory, here was a more adjustable set-up, although it has been the result of much confusion among players and repairers over the years, many of whom misunderstood the operation of the rods. As a result, a few discovered a new Rickenbacker feature, the pop-off fingerboard, while others found neck cracks. Rickenbacker eventually simplified its truss-rod system in 1984.

By July 1957, Rickenbacker's pricelist showed a respectable line-up of nine electric Spanish models: the Combo 850 at $279.50 (in turquoise blue; an extra $10 for natural maple); the Combo 800 at $279.50 (blond or turquoise blue); the Combo 650 $217.50 (turquoise blue; plus $10 for natural); Combo 600 $229.50 (blond or turquoise blue); Combo 450 $179.50 (jet black, cloverfield green, or montezuma brown); Combo 400 $159.50 (colours as 450); Model 950 $149.50, Model 900 $114.50, and the Model 1000 at $104.50 (the last three all jet black).

Around this time, Paul Barth left Rickenbacker. He went on to work in various small guitar-making operations, including his own Barth company and at Magnatone in the late 50s as well as Bartell in the 60s. At Rickenbacker, Ward Deaton replaced Barth as factory manager at the Los Angeles factory, where he headed up a team of around a dozen workers, including foreman Bill Myers. Roger Rossmeisl continued as 'chief designer' (although official job titles did not exist) and had a number of assistants working under him, including Semie Moseley, who came and went in the late 50s. Moseley later set up his Mosrite company, best known for the Ventures model played by that 60s instrumental group. It had some design features that recall the work of Rossmeisl. Another of Rossmeisl's assistants then was Dick Burke, who joined Rickenbacker in March 1958. He proved to be a long-standing employee at Rickenbacker, finally retiring in 2000.

Toward the end of 1958, Rickenbacker issued two new solid models with a new body shape. The body of the single-pickup 425 ($149.50) and two-pickup 450 ($184.50) had a hooked upper horn, lending the guitar a 'cresting wave' shape across the two cutaways. Since then, Rickenbacker has used this style on a number of its solid electric guitars and still uses it today.

In years to come, it would be clear that 1958 was an important year for Rickenbacker, which introduced a series of new models that formed the basis for its success during the 60s and beyond. These thin hollowbody electric guitar designs – known at first as the Capri series, named for the Hall family's cat – were largely the responsibility of Roger Rossmeisl.

Rossmeisl reacted primarily to directions from his superiors at Rickenbacker, as Dick Burke recalls. "If Mr Hall wanted something, Roger would try to come up with it," he says. "First off, he'd usually put a small sketch of it on paper."[17] Rossmeisl seems to have been a loner, happiest when working in isolation on a new design. He often tried to do most of

● At the 1956 trade shows, Rickenbacker emphasised its longevity by celebrating **25 years** since the original Frying Pan. A mix of visitors and booth babes (right) consider the history. A 1958 promo **postcard** (above) shows the new 'hooked' body on model 425.

FIRST IN 1931- FINEST IN 1956!

Model 900, 950 and 1000

Model 900   Model 950   Model 1000

The Model 900, 950, and 1000 three-quarter Spanish guitars are designed and engineered for lead or rhythm playing. Their lighter weight adds to the ease of playing and the portability of the instrument. Good quality tone is assured with the use of a specially designed Rickenbacker pickups, separate volume and tone controls, and tone control switch. The neck, which extends from the patent heads to the base of the guitar, has a separate fingerboard mounted on it. The neck has a double metal adjusting rod and all strain from the strings is on one piece of wood assuring the player of a straight neck. The guitars are available with natural finish necks and Jet Black "cutaway" bodies with an attractive, durable white pickguard. The shoulder strap supplied with the guitar connects to the back of the guitar with a single hook, allowing greater ease in handling the guitar and enabling the player to make quick changes from one instrument to another. The instrument used is also indicated.

The MODEL 900 guitar has a full 21-fret fingerboard scaled to fit the average player's fingers.

The MODEL 950 guitar is identical to the 900 with an additional pickup unit and 3-position tone switch.

The MODEL 1000 is also identical to the Model 900, except the curved, natural finish fingerboard has 18 frets instead of 21 for those who do not require the full scale.

● A first-year **Combo 850** (above) has the new "sweeping crescent" body shape that Rickenbacker introduced in 1957. Apart from the revised shape, everything else was similar to the existing Combo 800. The design would prove of great importance to Rickenbacker's future. Belgian-born guitarist **Jean "Toots" Thielemans** (below) was pictured in 1957 with a Combo 400, while two more trade-show visitors (bottom) that same year play a new-shape **Combo 450** (left) and old-style **Combo 650**.

● This 1957 **Model 1000** (main guitar) was the cheapest in a trio of short-scale "student" solidbodys introduced in 1957. As with the more upscale versions, these beginners' guitars employed through-neck construction. However, unlike its partner 900 and 950 models (**1957 catalogue**, above), the 1000 came with 18 frets instead of 21, and its shorter neck required a diffferent body style, akin to the more pronounced tulip shape found on models 400 and 450.

the jobs himself rather than delegating tasks to others. Another Rickenbacker man said that Rossmeisl was therefore not best suited to the team-work that a guitar factory demands – but that his talent for design could make up for any such shortcomings.

With the new electric hollowbody Capri guitars, more accurately described as semi-acoustics, Rossmeisl further developed the scooped-out construction he'd first used on some of the early Combo models. Rather than make a hollow guitar in the traditional acoustic method – where a flat, carved, or pressed top is secured to a back and rims – Rossmeisl designed the Capri models to be built from a solid block of wood, usually two halves of maple joined together. Wrokers would cut this to a rough body shape and then partially hollow out from the back. A separate wooden back was then added, once all the electric parts had been secured, and the neck was glued into place. It's certainly unusual – and to this day is pure Rickenbacker.

The first such Capri model that Rickenbacker announced was the small-body 325 model, a guitar that would have a great effect on the company's success when it was taken up a few years later by John Lennon. F.C. Hall regularly sent out General Sales Bulletins to thc Radio-Tel salesmen to keep them up to date with new product developments. In one such Bulletin, dated February 1958, Hall previewed the 325 model, which he described as "the first item in the Capri series hollowbody guitars".

Hall continued: "Others have made combination models of acoustic and electric. … Our model is made strictly as an electric guitar but has all the qualities of the solidbody models. The hollowbody has definite advantages in many respects over solidbody electric guitars. First of all, it is lighter in weight which makes it easier to handle – it only weighs five-and-a-quarter pounds. It is thicker, so it looks more like an acoustic guitar. Also, the body is two inches longer than the bodies used on our Model 900 and 1000 series. The body on the new model measures 16 x 13 x 2 inches.

"The bodies and necks are attractively finished in a natural finish similar to our Combo 850 … . We are also introducing for the first time a brown two-toned finish, sometimes called Sunburst, which adds considerable class to the appearance of the guitar for those who wish a darker finish.

"Furthermore, we have made this model with the three-quarter neck, which many professionals feel is much easier to play than the standard conventional length neck. Also, it is easier for a student or a person with a small hand to play the new model as the fingering is closer together." The point about the short-scale neck was lost on pro players. Quite simply, the cramped confines of short-scale guitars make them harder to play by those with full-scale hands.

Hall went on to mention the 325's three chrome-plated pickups, its "famous" Kauffman vibrato unit (with a cautionary note about the danger of detuning the strings through extreme use), and the guitar's "full cutaway" for access to the 21st fret. Hall's note to his salesmen concluded by quoting a list price for the forthcoming Capri 325 of "only $249.50 without the case". He concluded: "I am sure you will not find another guitar with all of these features, precision balanced, near this price." Gibson's fancy three-pickup Les Paul Custom listed at $375 in 1958, and Fender's Stratocaster at $274.50.

Another Rickenbacker feature highlighted by the Capri models was a very slim neck, achieved in combination with the company's double-truss-rod system – and later Rickenbacker's distinctive glossy lacquered fingerboard was added. These models also began to appear with two now-classic Rickenbacker design elements: 'toaster-top' pickups, nicknamed for their split chrome look; and two-tier pickguards, at first in an arresting gold-coloured plastic. The split guards had a base plate flush to the guitar's body, carrying the controls, and a separate guard raised on three short pillars, intended as a finger-rest.

Later in February 1958, a further General Sales Bulletin from Hall made the first mention of "full length Capri guitars". Hall told his salesmen that this style of instrument, a full-size version of the small-body 325 type, "will be available at least as a sample to you some time in April". His deadpan prediction would certainly turn out to be accurate: "It will be a very popular guitar," concluded Hall.

The full 12-model Capri Series was detailed on Rickenbacker's June 1958 pricelist, under three headings: *Three-quarter necks:* 310 $224.50 (two pickups, two-tone brown or natural finish); 315 $239.50 (as 310 but with vibrato); 320 $239.50 (as 310 but three pickups); and 325 $249.50 (as 310 but three pickups and vibrato).

Full-necks: 330 $259.50 (two pickups, two-tone brown or natural finish); 335 $274.50 (as 330 but with vibrato); 340 $274.50 (as 330 but three pickups); 345 $289.50 (as 330 but three pickups and vibrato).

Deluxe full-necks: 360 $309.50 (two pickups, two-tone brown with white binding or natural with brown binding, triangle fingerboard inlays); 365 $329.50 (as 360 but with vibrato); 370 $329.50 (as 360 but three pickups); 375 $348.50 (as 360 but three pickups and vibrato).

Meanwhile, the July 1958 issue of *The Music Trades* magazine publicly announced the 12-model Capri line for launch to dealers at the National Association of Music Merchants (NAMM) trade show that summer in Chicago.

Some of the hardware used on the original Capris furthered the idiosyncratic nature of the guitars, most notably Rickenbacker's distinctive control knobs with diamond-shaped pointers on top. These large knobs would have looked equally at home on kitchen ovens of the period, which is why many collectors call them cooker knobs. The vibrato-equipped models were fitted with the quirky Kauffman units, which remained awkward and flimsy and had a distinct tendency to render the strings out-of-tune after even delicate use. The Kauffmans did at least look different.

The Capri guitars were curvaceous and stylish, a testament to the design sense of the German-born Rossmeisl. Some of the apparently new elements would have seemed more familiar when considered in the context of contemporary German guitar design, especially the inclusion on many Rickenbacker models of the dramatic scimitar-shaped soundhole (since nicknamed the 'slash' soundhole), the triangular fingerboard inlays on deluxe models,

Fast play neck

21 FRETS WITHIN EASIER, FASTER REACH THAN EVER BEFORE — ON THE RICKENBACKER SPANISH GUITAR

- Rickenbacker offers the neck that is "precision contoured" to fit the hand in any fingering position.
- Rickenbacker has the uniformly slim neck, from top to bottom, that speeds play by reducing hand position changes.
- Rickenbacker's exclusive, deep "cut-away" body, makes frets close to the body easier to reach, easier to play.

Rickenbacker
SPANISH GUITAR

"Most respected name in Guitars, Amplifiers and Accessories."

Distributed exclusively by
RADIO & TELEVISION EQUIPMENT COMPANY
2118 South Main Street, Santa Ana, California

● Rickenbacker and Roger Rossmeisl's masterstroke was the design for the **Capri** series, introduced in 1958. The shape and style suited a large body (three examples, left) or a small one (a first-year **325** is featured in the photo above). These designs, with some modifications, would prove to be the most important in Rickenbacker's history. In the meantime, the company set about promoting the new guitars with a stylish **catalogue** in 1959 (below) and an **advertisement** (right) that pushed the advantages of the slim neck and playability of these hollowbody instruments.

Rickenbacker
The World's Most Distinguished Name in Guitars, Amplifiers and Accessories
SPANISH GUITARS

● Three fabulous Capris: 1959 **360** (top); 1958 **330** (centre), and 1959 **365** (main guitar). Classic Rickenbacker features are in place: toaster-top pickups, slash soundhole, cooker knobs, and triangle markers for the deluxe models. Francis Hall's photos show his wife Catherine (top) with a new **325** and a friend with a gorgeous **365** (opposite).

and an elegant recess carved in the lower front of the body to accommodate the tailpiece.

During 1958, Rickenbacker added a Thick Body model to the full-scale Capri series, featuring a lavishly carved, deep body. Here again, Rossmeisl's German heritage was evident – the raised 'shoulder' running parallel to the edge of the body on these guitars is known as a German carve, a typical feature of the work of some German guitar-makers, including Roger and his father Wenzel. Despite detailing 14 different electric and acoustic Thick Body models on its July 1958 pricelist, Rickenbacker in fact only produced one German-carve electric model, the two-pickup 381, which listed at $498.

As if all this wasn't enough, in 1958 Rickenbacker launched yet another addition to the Capri line. If anything, the Thin Full-Body series was rather more conventional than the rest of the newcomers. These guitars had a 'thin' cross-section, like the 310–375 Capri models, but their 'full' body was larger in outline, and they boasted a single rounded cutaway like some other guitars of the period, including a number of Gibson's contemporary ES models.

Rickenbacker gave these Thin Full-Body models an F suffix, and they first appeared on the company's April 1959 pricelist. Dick Burke recalls that there were some problems with body cracks on the F instruments, and production appears to have been relatively modest. The pricelist notes that the guitars were officially available in the standard two-tone brown or natural finishes, as follows: 330F $249.50 (two pickups); 335F $274.50 (as 330F but with vibrato); 340F $274.50 (three pickups); 345F $289.50 (as 340F but with vibrato); 360F $299 (two pickups, bound body and neck, triangle-shaped fingerboard inlays); 365F $329.50 (as 360F but with vibrato); 370F $329.50 (three pickups, bound body and neck, triangle fingerboard inlays); 375F $348.50 (as 370F but with vibrato).

During the course of 1960 in Liverpool, England, a three-man guitar group of great ambition if little activity dropped their original name of The Quarry Men and, after a number of variations, decided to call themselves The Beatles. They added a bass player and then a drummer to the original trio, and in August their almost-but-not-quite-manager Allan Williams remarkably secured the under-rehearsed group a run of 48 nights at the Indra club in Hamburg, northern Germany.

The Beatles took their basic instruments and equipment with them for what turned out to be a gruelling engagement, shifting in October to the Kaiserkeller club. George Harrison had a Futurama, a cheap Czech-made guitar. Bassist Stuart Sutcliffe worked with a big German Hofner 333 bass, while Paul McCartney, still a guitarist for now, played an undistinguished Dutch-made Rosetti Solid 7 model. John Lennon got by on a £28 Hofner Club 40 electric hollowbody guitar.

Lennon bought a Rickenbacker 325 while he was in Hamburg. It must have looked magnificent compared to the guitars the group were used to. "I sold my Hofner, made a profit on it too, and bought one," Lennon said a few years later. He called his Rickenbacker "the most beautiful guitar" and added that the action "is really ridiculously low".[18] George Harrison remembered going to a music store in Hamburg with Lennon to buy the guitar and that it was the first Rickenbacker he'd ever seen. Harrison said that Lennon bought the 325 from the Steinway music store in Hamburg, although local research suggests that the guitar may have been acquired from the nearby Musikhaus Rotthoff.

"I bought a Gibson amplifier and John bought that little Rickenbacker," Harrison said later. "I think he'd just seen an album by Jean 'Toots' Thielemans, who used to be guitar player in the George Shearing Quintet and had one of those Rickenbackers." It may have been in Hamburg that Lennon saw Thielemans playing a Rickenbacker. Certainly the Belgian guitarist and harmonica-player worked in Germany in 1960, probably with Kurt Edelhagen's radio orchestra among others.

Whichever Hamburg shop window it was hanging in, that good-quality US-made Rickenbacker 325 was, Harrison confirmed, an almost unbelievable sight to the pair of raw Liverpudlian musicians. "You have to imagine that in those days, when we were first out of Liverpool, any good American guitar looked sensational to us. We'd only had beat-up crummy guitars at that stage. We still didn't really have any money to buy them, but I remember that John got that Rickenbacker and I got this amplifier. And we got them what they call 'on the knocker', you know? [Money] down and the rest when they catch you! I don't know if we ever really paid them off."

Harrison recalled that Lennon made the purchase "purely because [he] needed a decent guitar, and that one happened to be in the shop and he liked the look of it".[19] The instrument had certainly been around a while: its serial number indicated it was made in 1958.

Lennon's 325 was finished in natural maple and at first had the standard 'cooker' knobs and Kauffman vibrato, but neither was apparently to Lennon's liking. The knobs he replaced quickly with smaller Hofner types, while the Kauffman he replaced with a more efficient Bigsby vibrato unit – and in late 1962 he had the guitar refinished from the original natural colour to black. This first Beatle Rickenbacker would not be the last.

Meanwhile, back in sunny California, the Rickenbacker team had their hands full with the new semi-acoustic range – no longer called Capri after 1959 – as well as the solidbody lines. Salesman Joe Talbot remembered some of the efforts they made to market these new Rickenbacker guitars to music store owners around the country. Talbot worked as southern-states salesman for Rickenbacker between 1959 and 1961. Rickenbacker boss F.C. Hall met Talbot, who had played guitar with Hank Snow, through steel guitarist Jerry Byrd, a long-standing Rickenbacker devotee.

Talbot took to the road with a Capri 365 and a Rickenbacker amplifier to demonstrate the new line to his customers in Texas, Oklahoma, Tennessee, and surrounding states. "I only called on larger towns, because the smaller towns had maybe one music store with all the big lines and didn't have any necessity for a new line," he recalled. "But in the bigger towns you could find a music store that did not have all the well-known lines and might have a need for another line of guitars and amplifiers.

"Most of them thought the model 365 was a beautiful, gorgeous guitar. First time or two around I'm not sure that they were sold on them. It was kind of new to them, though

● Another new line for 1958 was the **Thin Full Body** series – thin in depth, like the regular 300 models, but fuller bodied, a little more conventional, and given an F suffix. A 360F was shown off in the 1959 catalogue (third from left, above) and a 365F in a stylish **ad** from the same year (right).

● This 1960 **375F** (below) has a Germanic feel to the design, again reflecting Roger Rossmeisl's involvement. There were eight models in the "F" line, with the deluxe-featured 375F at the top. The "5" at the end of the model number means "with vibrato".

● **John Lennon** bought his **Rickenbacker 325** when The Beatles were in Hamburg, Germany in 1960. He's pictured with it (above) in December 1961 at the Cavern in Liverpool. Lennon made changes, replacing the original vibrato with a Bigsby and adding new knobs, and in 1962 he refinished it in black. Rickenbacker gave him a new 325 in 1964, but his first 325 is seen (right) as it is today in the care of Yoko Ono, its body restored to the original natural.

people did know Rickenbacker – they were better known then for the Hawaiian guitars. But this time around, Rickenbacker had this gorgeous, new, very complete line, from small solidbodies right up to big hollowbodies. I had a full catalogue with pictures of everything and a brief description. The dealers' attitude wasn't negative, it was more, 'Well, let me wait and see.' If the store had someone in it that was a guitar player, they would compare the 365 to the other guitars they had. Those that did not play evaluated it more on its appearance – and it was impressive."[20]

Talbot said Rickenbacker's main competition at the time was Fender, which he described as "that sound that everybody was after". Gibson's new thinline semi-acoustic electric launched in 1958, the ES-335, was selling well too, but the loyal Talbot did not think it was much of a competitor for Rickenbacker's guitars.

Rickenbacker's workers were busy making some modifications to the guitar lines. From about 1960, the existing two-tone brown sunburst finish was officially called autumnglo, and a new red-to-yellow sunburst option began to appear, officially named fireglo. A reliable new serial-numbering system was established in 1960 – it's explained in the reference section at the back of this book – and a new stereo-output feature called Rick-O-Sound was added to some guitars, usually the 'deluxe' models, from around the summer of that year.

Rick-O-Sound exploited the new interest at the time in two-channel stereophonic sound, consolidated in 1958 when most of the big recording companies began issuing stereo records. Gretsch and then Gibson launched 'stereo' guitars and Rickenbacker decided to follow suit. The company's system simply separated the output from the neck pickup and the bridge pickup, with a special split cable feeding the individual signals to two amplifiers (or to two channels of one amplifier).

This pseudo-stereo feature was made possible by a special double jack plate fitted to Rick-O-Sound models. One output was marked 'Standard', and when an ordinary mono cable was plugged in here, a switch contact inside disconnected the stereo circuit and provided regular guitar output. The output marked 'Rick-O-Sound' required a stereo plug connected to a Y cable. Rickenbacker offered this as an accessory with an interconnection box, rather grandly called the Rick-O-Sound Kit, for $24.50 (it first appeared on the July 1960 pricelist).

In many cases, guitarists used instruments with Rick-O-Sound as usual in mono and ignored the extra facility. Salesman Joe Talbot recalled the introduction of the stereo feature. "I frankly don't remember there being that much response to it, simply because it required more investment – you had to have two amplifiers."

It was also around this time that Rickenbacker decided to replace the unpredictable Kauffman unit with a new vibrato, the Ac'cent. Although by no means a sophisticated or especially sturdy vibrato, it was at least an improvement on the Kauffman. The Ac'cent uses a sprung steel plate attached to a tailpiece section. Pressure on a bent metal arm affects spring tension, providing the vibrato effect.

Talbot remembered coming across a sample of the Ac'cent in a music store in Texas, probably in 1960, and writing to F.C. Hall about this potential replacement for the problematic Kauffman. Talbot was getting complaints about the old vibrato from his customers. "People found it hard to keep the guitar in tune with that one – it drove me crazy."[21] The next time Talbot was at Rickenbacker HQ in Santa Ana, he and Hall travelled to San Diego to see the maker of the Ac'cent units, and Hall soon completed a deal for Rickenbacker to use them on its guitars, beginning around 1961.

The earliest units have "Ac'cent By Paul" on the steel plate. As well as employing them on vibrato models like the 325 and 335, Rickenbacker offered Ac'cents as add-on accessories for $42.50 each (first noted on the July 1961 pricelist). The Ac'cent was probably made by the same manufacturer who produced Gibson's similar Maestro Vibrola unit during the 60s.

Rickenbacker tried another new vibrato on a few guitars a year or so later. This was the Boyd Vibe, one of a few variations devised by Solon Boyd. But it was of poor design and didn't appear on many instruments nor for very long. Solon Boyd subsequently tried to market the Boyd Vibe separately, but even with an enthusiastic endorsement from Merle Travis it enjoyed little success.

In 1961, Rickenbacker introduced a deluxe guitar with the same body shape as the earlier 425, 450, and vibrato-equipped 615 and 625 models. The new 460 ($248.50) had triangle fingerboard markers, Rickenbacker's most obvious indicator of a deluxe model. More significantly, it was the first to carry the modified control layout the company would apply to nearly all its models over the coming years. On the 460, a fifth 'blend' control was added just behind the four regular controls, fitted with a smaller knob. The extra control was prompted by an idea that F.C. Hall had about tone circuits.

Consider the usual control set-up for a two-pickup guitar. There are individual volume and tone controls for each pickup, and a selector switch. The three-way selector offers: the pickup nearest the neck, with a more bassy tone, often used for rhythm playing; both pickups, balanced by the relative positions of the two volume controls; or the pickup nearest the bridge, with a toppier tone for lead playing. This is the control system that Rickenbacker used, too, but from 1961 it started to add the fifth knob to many models.

With the three-way selector in the neck-pickup-only or bridge-pickup-only position, the fifth knob is designed to provide the opportunity to blend in some tone from the unselected pickup. For example, with just the bassier neck pickup selected, the fifth knob allows you to blend in a little of the bridge pickup's treble tone. And vice versa. If the selector is in the middle position – in other words, giving both pickups – then the fifth knob allows you to vary the precise balance between the two, for increased tonal emphasis. The later development of modern channel-switching amplifiers made the fifth knob redundant for some players, but aside from this it does offer some increased versatility to the available tones.

On Rickenbackers fitted with the Rick-O-Sound stereo feature, the fifth knob functions more as a balance control between left and right – neck pickup and bridge pickup – because to achieve stereo the selector would be lodged in the centre position, so that both pickups are 'on'.

Some musicians have found the 'blend' knob baffling and decide to forget their guitar has it. Beatle George Harrison sounded exasperated when he spoke of his confusion. "That tiny little knob never seemed to do anything," he said in 1987. "All it ever seemed to be was that there was one sound that I could get where it was bright, which was the sound I used, and another tone where it all went muffled, which I never used."[22]

Tom Petty heard the same argument from Harrison. "He used to tell me that it didn't do anything. I said, yes it does! He'd say no, I couldn't ever get mine to do anything. And I said, well, yours is broken then, because it does do something. It adds bottom in or out, simple as that. Do it carefully enough, and you can get a really nice sound."[23]

Rickenbacker was busy during the summer of 1962 moving its factory from South Western Avenue, Los Angeles – where the guitars had been made since the 30s – down to Kilson Drive, Santa Ana, not far from the Radio-Tel headquarters. Rickenbacker's team was finding it increasingly tiresome to shift new guitars the 35 miles or so from Los Angeles to the distribution centre in Santa Ana. Especially F.C. Hall's wife Catherine, who generally took charge of such business. "I lived near Santa Ana," F.C. recalled, "so the move consolidated things and cut down some of the overheads."

Dick Burke, who'd worked for the company for four years, also remembers welcoming the move in 1962. "I wanted to get out of LA," he says. "Santa Ana was real small at that time, there were no freeways about, and I liked the country. I think we had about the same factory space at the new place, but the actual buildings were bigger."

Most of the dozen or so workers stayed on after the move south, but soon afterward Roger Rossmeisl left the company and went to work for Fender in Fullerton (about 15 miles away), hired primarily to work on a new line of acoustic guitars. More than any other single person, it was Rossmeisl who created the classic Rickenbacker look, and despite his sometimes unorthodox methods, Rossmeisl's departure must have been a blow to the company. Burke says that Rossmeisl was already planning to leave when the factory was moved and had by that stage bought a new house nearer to the Fender plant. Rossmeisl stayed at Fender until about 1968. He eventually returned to his native Germany, and he died there in 1979 at the age of just 52.

Rickenbacker's July 1962 pricelist showed the current line-up of 32 electric models, split into four groups. *Combo Series, Solid Bodies:* 425 $179.50; 450 $249.50; 460 $299 (last three in black, natural, or fireglo finish); 600 (blond or turquoise blue) $179.50; 615 (fireglo) $329.50; 625 $359.50 (black, natural, or fireglo); 800 (turquoise blue) $215; 850 (turquoise blue or natural) $225; 900 $139.50; 950 $169.50; 1000 $129.50 (last three black, natural, or fireglo).

310–375 Series, Thin Hollow Bodies (fireglo or natural): 310 $294.50; 315 $344.50; 320 $309.50 ; 325 $359.50; 330 $319.50; 335 $369.50; 340 $339.50; 345 $384.50; 360 $394.50;

365 $439.50; 370 $409.50; 375 $459.50. *F Series, Thin Full Hollow Bodies* (fireglo or natural): 330F $344.50; 335F $399.50; 340F $359.50; 345F $399.50; 360F $419.50; 365F $474.50; 370F $439.50; 375F $489.50. *Thick Body Series* (autumnglo or natural): 381 $498.

In the meantime, F.C. Hall and his colleagues at Rickenbacker decided to develop an electric 12-string during 1963. There had been three earlier attempts at a similar type of instrument – more of which in a moment.

Guitar-like instruments with paired strings ('courses' is the technical term) go back much further. If you're historically minded, you might want to go all the way back to the lute, which through its long history appeared with anything from four to ten or more courses: some paired, some single.

The lute is related to another ancient stringed instrument with paired courses, the Middle-Eastern ud, and the Greek bouzouki that was something like a large mandolin and usually had four courses.

Early guitars, too, had paired courses, gradually developing around the mid 1500s from the original four courses to five and to six in the late 1700s. The guitar family branches out to include such wonders as the Mexican–Texan 12-string bajo sexto (with string pairs tuned in fourths) and the Brazilian 10-string viola caipira (often open-tuned).

In the United States, flat-top acoustic 12-string guitars first appeared around 1900. These had six paired courses. Lyon & Healy of Chicago was best known for the Washburn brand, but its model 1860 12-string, advertised as "Mexican Style", bore the Lakeside brand. Around the same time, Holzapfel & Beitel in Baltimore, Grunewald in New Orleans, Charles Bruno in New York City, and Oscar Schmidt in Jersey City were all selling 12-string guitars. Schmidt's 12s included Stella-brand models, and these budget-price guitars with their big clanging sound were made famous in the early decades of the 20th century by bluesmen such as Blind Willie McTell and, most notably, Leadbelly.

The folk boom of the early 60s in the US and elsewhere revived interest in acoustic 12s, their big sound providing many an unsure singer with a helpful boost. All the best-known guitar brands introduced a flat-top 12-string model or two to meet the demand, including Gibson (in 1961), Guild (1964), and Martin (1964). In Britain, many young guitarists of the 60s and 70s first discovered the power of acoustic 12 thanks to the popular Italian-made Eko brand. Of course, some players experimented by adding a pickup to their acoustic, and while that made for a louder result, it wasn't the same as a purpose-built electric 12.

One of the leading figures in the folk revival was Pete Seeger, who played an acoustic 12 made for him by Stan Francis – the same Liverpool-based maker whose guitar had delighted George Harrison.

Hit folk records spread the big sound of the 12, none more so than 'Walk Right In' by The Rooftop Singers, which at the start of 1963 took the 12-string folk sound right up to Number 1 in the US pop charts and into the British Top 10. Erik Darling and Bill Svanoe of the Rooftops pitched two Gibson 12-strings at the heart of the record's driving sound.

The acoustic 12-string established a tuning system that would be adopted by the later electric versions. There are four pairs of strings each with a normally-tuned string – the regular E, A, D, and G – plus a string an octave higher, and two pairs – the B and high E – each with two identical strings tuned in unison. This strengthening of the guitar's sound through octave and unison doubling produces the classic jangling 12-string sound, almost as if two guitars are playing together. On most 12-string guitars, acoustic or electric, the fatter regular string is below the octave string, looking down from the player's viewpoint. As we'll see, one guitar-maker would make a significant change to that unwritten rule.

An interesting adaptation of the acoustic 12-string sound is known as Nashville tuning. Think of it as a 6-string guitar strung with only the high strings of a 12-string set. The two highest strings remain as a regular 6-string – they're in unison on a 12-string – while the four lower strings are the octave strings of the 12-string set. The result is a high, ringing sound, and doubled with a regular 6-string it provides a strengthened 12-string-like sound.

But what of the electric 12-string – and those three pre-Rickenbacker examples? The first electric 12-string guitar was introduced as one half of a strange double-neck guitar, the Stratosphere Twin, designed around 1954 by Russ and Claude Deaver in Springfield, Missouri. The lower neck was a regular 6-string, but the upper neck was a 12-string, tuned in a very unusual way and intended to provide the owner with a harmony twin-guitar lead sound – without the irksome need for a second guitarist. The Stratosphere Guitar Mfg Co also featured a $139.50 single-neck 12-string model in its catalogue, although it's doubtful if that one went into production.

"Excitingly new! Astonishingly different! The guitar of tomorrow … today!" exclaimed the catalogue. Deke Dickerson, a musician, writer, and guitar historian who has studied the Stratosphere story, explains: "The tuning system of the Stratosphere 12-string was a bizarre code, akin to deciphering Egyptian hieroglyphics. Three pairs of strings were tuned to major thirds and three pairs to minor thirds. In addition, the guitar was not tuned EADGBE like a standard guitar but FADFAC (low to high) with the harmony strings tuned ACFACE. Essentially, those who wanted to accomplish this miracle of twin-guitar leads on one guitar had to re-learn the instrument from scratch."

Chet Atkins obviously thought otherwise. He recorded both sides of a 1955 single, 'Shine On Harvest Moon' and 'Somebody Stole My Gal', with the Twin 12-string in regular octave tuning, so that he could fingerpick – the harmony tuning didn't work for chordal playing. The Stratosphere catalogue also mentioned an odd lower-pitch octave tuning.

The man who made the Stratosphere Twin his own, even if briefly, was Jimmy Bryant. He's best known today for the astonishing instrumental duet records he made back in the 50s with pedal-steel virtuoso Speedy West. Bryant was a busy Hollywood session player and a regular on Cliffie Stone's TV country showcase, *Hometown Jamboree*. He was always keen to try the latest guitar gear and for example had been among the first to publicly play Leo Fender's solidbody electric Broadcaster.

Bryant jumped at the chance to use the Twin 12-string double-neck, to play what Stratosphere described as "double-string lead as fast as you would ordinarily play single-string lead". With Bryant, however, nothing was ever anywhere near ordinary. He played the new guitar on a 1954 Bryant–West single, the remarkable A-side of which is aptly titled 'Stratosphere Boogie'. It's dominated by Bryant's swooping, rolling 12-string solos.

"Jimmy created a tour de force that could never be duplicated," says Deke Dickerson. "'Stratosphere Boogie' was so fast, so clean, and so masterful that the majority of the listening audience really didn't know what was going on." Bryant also played his Twin on the gentler B-side, 'Deep Water'.

"It's tempting, in today's video-oriented world, to think that the Stratosphere Twin might have caused a sensation," says Dickerson. "However, no one could tell what Jimmy Bryant was doing on 'Stratosphere Boogie', and for the average player the new tuning system was impossible to learn. The Twin was too far ahead of its time. Despite its best efforts, the Stratosphere company was out of business by 1958 or 1959 after making fewer than 200 instruments."[24]

Gibson certainly noticed the Stratosphere Twin before it disappeared. In 1958, the giant Michigan-based guitar maker produced its first two double-neck models, one of which, the EDS-1275 Double 12, had a regular six-string lower neck and a 12-string upper neck, just like the Twin. Gibson too suggested a couple of possible tunings.

"A completely new and exciting instrument," was the familiar phrase in Gibson's catalogue. "Six strings double-strung which can be tuned either in thirds or an octave apart for reinforced resonance and unusual tone effects." A note at the end added that the new Gibson double-neck was "custom-built to order only". Gibson produced just 110 Double 12s during the model's original ten-year life, including a shift from the original hollowbody style to a revised solidbody design in 1962. Nobody well-known played one at the time.

The third pre-Rickenbacker electric 12-string was also the first single-neck of our trio – but aside from that it could hardly be described as conventional. The New Jersey-based guitar maker Danelectro, which successfully produced decent budget-price instruments, teamed up with New York sessionman Vinnie Bell to make an unusual guitar they named the Bellzouki.

Howard Daniel, son of Danelectro's founder Nat Daniel, says that the instrument was inspired by the 1960 movie *Never On Sunday*.[25] This Greek film won an Oscar for best song, a first for a foreign-made film. As well as vocalist Melina Mercouri, star of *Never On Sunday*, the song also featured the ringing sound of a bouzouki. This is the traditional Greek stringed instrument, the modern version of which is often electric and usually features four paired strings – and sounds not unlike a rather metallic 12-string guitar.

The Danelectro Bellzouki – the name combines Vinnie Bell's surname with the last bit of bouzouki – became available around 1962 and first appeared in Danelectro's 1963 catalogue. The one-pickup 7010 version did have something of the look of a bouzouki,

Played and recommended by **JIMMY BRYANT**, West Coast Radio, Television and Capital Recording Artist.
The "Stratosphere Boogie" and "Deep Water" are his latest hits.

● The first electric 12-string guitar was the **Stratosphere Twin** of 1955 (main guitar), a double-neck with 12 and 6-string. It was designed by Russ and Claude Deaver, who ran the small Stratosphere firm in Missouri. The Twin was shortlived, but its finest player was Hollywood sessionman **Jimmy Bryant** (top). In the early 60s, Rickenbacker introduced the **460** model (below), the first with a fifth "blend" knob, and **Rick-O-Sound** stereo output (top left).

42

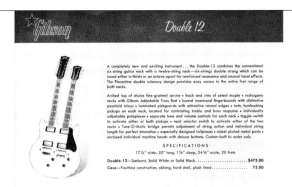

Double 12

A completely new and exciting instrument... the Double-12 combines the conventional six-string guitar neck with a twelve-string neck—six-strings double strung which can be tuned either in thirds or an octave apart for reinforced resonance and unusual tonal effects. The Florentine double cutaway design provides easy access to the entire fret range of both necks.

Arched top of choice fine-grained spruce • back and rims of select maple • mahogany necks with Gibson Adjustable Truss Rod • bound rosewood fingerboards with distinctive pearloid inlays • laminated pickguards with attractive reveal edges • twin, humbucking pickups on each neck, located for contrasting treble and bass response • individually adjustable polepieces • separate tone and volume controls for each neck • toggle switch to activate either or both pickups • neck selector switch to activate either of the two necks • Tune-O-Matic bridge permits adjustment of string action and individual string length for perfect intonation • especially designed tailpieces • nickel plated metal parts • enclosed individual machine heads with deluxe buttons. Custom-built to order only.

SPECIFICATIONS
17¼" wide, 20" long, 1⅝" deep, 24¾" scale, 20 frets

Double-12—Sunburst, Solid White or Solid Black.........................$475.00
Case—Faultless construction, oblong, hard shell, plush lined................. 75.00

● Gibson took note of the Stratosphere Twin and came up with its own double-neck model, the **EDS-1275 Double 12**, which was first shown in Gibson's 1958 catalogue (above). It turned out to be a rare model in its original guise, with just over 100 made of this original hollowbody and the later solidbody, which was introduced in 1962. Meanwhile, Rickenbacker introduced on a few models what turned out to be a shortlived vibrato,

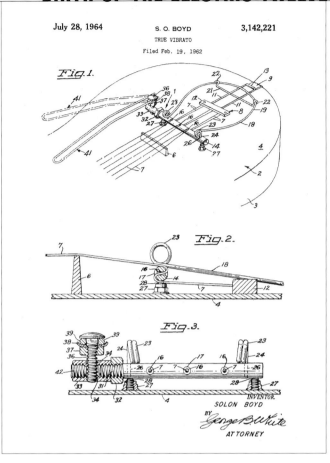

July 28, 1964   S. O. BOYD   3,142,221
TRUE VIBRATO
Filed Feb. 19, 1962

Fig. 1.

Fig. 2.

Fig. 3.

INVENTOR.
SOLON BOYD
BY
George B. White
ATTORNEY

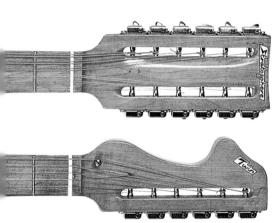

● **Acoustic 12-string** guitars had been around for many years, but the folk boom of the early 60s brought a new popularity to the big sound of the 12. **Leadbelly** with his Stella 12-string (below left) was a big influence, while one of the new folk stars was **Pete Seeger**, pictured (below) with his 12-string guitar custom-made by Stan Francis.

with a large-mandolin-like rounded body, while the two-pickup model 7020 was a little more ornate. Both models had a splayed six-tuners-each-side headstock. "They evoke the mysterious charm and flavor of remote times and places, yet are easily played using familiar guitar technique," claimed Danelectro.

Naturally, Bell took one along with his other guitars for his busy studio schedule. One of the earliest sessions on which he played the Bellzouki was Paul Anka's 'A Steel Guitar And A Glass Of Wine', creating a distinctive and very bouzouki-like jangle at the start of the song (and, oddly, nothing like a steel guitar). Anka's single went to Number 13 in the US in June 1962 and was probably the first American hit record with an electric 12-string, even if musicians who heard it probably just assumed it featured a real bouzouki.

Bell's first solo album *Whistle Stop*, recorded in late 1963 and released early the following year, was designed to show off his cutting-edge effects. To our jaded 21st century ears, Bell might sound rather tame as he deploys distortion, echo, volume, and delay on the record's 12-bars and covers. But the results had the Verve label calling him "the dreamer behind this fantastic array of new sounds" and warning the listener to "toss out every idea you've ever had about what a guitar should sound like".

Bell plays his Bellzouki electric 12-string on two tracks. For 'I Have But One Heart' it's the same fast-strumming faux-Greek sound he used on the Anka single. On 'Bellzouki', however, he goes for strong 12-string lines and riffs, an early take on the sound that would soon have pop guitarists lining up to use electric 12-strings on their own records.

During 1963 F.C. Hall, no doubt aware of the attempts by Gibson, Danelectro, and Stratosphere, began to wonder if an electric 12-string would make a good new product for Rickenbacker. He asked Dick Burke, head of the company's woodshop at the time, to find a way for a 12-string system to work with Rickenbacker's existing designs.

Burke considered the classic big-bodied 360 style for the new 12-string model. He tried to find a way of incorporating the necessary 12 tuners into a headstock the same size as Rickenbacker's regular six-string guitars. Other 12-string guitars tended to range six tuners along each side of a necessarily elongated headstock. Despite a prototype with exactly that kind of long headstock – and six rear-facing banjo tuners – Hall thought it looked ungainly and encouraged Burke to find a solution.

Burke looked at the options. "I drilled around," he remembers, "and we worked it different ways." The scheme he came up with was brilliantly simple, an imaginative leap that solved the problem Hall had posed and, in the process, created an attractive and ingenious piece of guitar design.

He kept the existing six tuners where they normally were – three on each side of the headstock. He then routed two parallel channels into the face of the headstock – like the slots on a classical guitar but not going all the way through. Burke attached the second set of six tuners at 90 degrees to the first set, the keys facing 'backwards' – again, like a classical guitar, with strings attached into the tuners' spindles in the channels – and gently altered the overall outline.

"That headstock didn't take very long to come up with," he says, modestly. "We thought about putting the rout all the way through, in fact I think I made a couple like that, but it looked better without. We ended up with a rout just a little way in."[26]

Rickenbacker made three experimental 12-string guitars in 1963. The first, a 360-style instrument, was fitted with a gold-coloured pickguard and what collectors now call cooker knobs – attractive art deco-style controls with a diamond-shape gold pointer insert in a black top. The guitar had the higher string of the octave pairs nearest the player, just like the regular system used by most makers of 12-string acoustic guitars.

The two further prototype Rickenbacker 12-strings made in 1963 were another 360 and a model 620-style guitar, both fitted with the white pickguard and black knobs that the company was introducing at the time. These two instruments had what became Rickenbacker's standard stringing method for 12-string guitars, placing the octave string beyond the regular 'fatter' string of each pair, from the player's point of view. With this idiosyncratic arrangement, the player's downstroke hits that lower string before the octave string, giving a slightly different sound.

Rickenbacker's first 12-string, the one with the gold pickguard, went to Suzi Arden, a showband singer, fiddle-player, and guitarist. The Suzi Arden Show was a regular at the Golden Nugget and the Mint Hotel's Merri Mint Lounge in Las Vegas.

When Arden visited the Rickenbacker offices in November 1963, the company provided her country-oriented band with Rickenbacker amplifiers, with the three back-up guitarists – including Leon and Ray Richardson – receiving Rickenbacker guitars and a bass. "Mr Hall brought me the 12-string," Arden remembers. "It was the first one, his 'model'. He always brought me new things he was doing. He said to try this new 12-string out and see how you like it. I did, and I wouldn't let him take it back," she laughs.

"I was playing a Martin electric six-string at the time," Arden continues, "but the Rickenbacker was so sweet, sounded so good, and it added to my show so much. It made a sharp, beautiful sound – there's nothing I think sounds as beautiful as a Rickenbacker 12. I could play all the chords on it real easy, and being electric, also, I loved it. I used the 12-string always from that point on, for the next 20-something years."[27]

Having made the three 12-string samples, and with one in active use, Rickenbacker must have been sure by the end of 1963 that such an instrument would make a viable addition to its line for 1964.

Around this time, F.C. Hall worked on some correspondence from an overseas firm keen to do business, no doubt a regular chore for the boss. But this contact would turn out to be an important one. Managers at London-based Rose, Morris & Co Ltd (better known by its later name, Rose-Morris) had first written to Rickenbacker back in July 1962 to enquire about selling the California company's products in the UK. Rickenbacker had exported products before, but for the moment Hall did little to follow up the proposal.

During 1963, Rose-Morris again contacted Hall about importing Rickenbacker guitars. Hall received similar enquiries from at least two other British operations: Jennings, who

● Another early electric 12-string was the **Danelectro Bellzouki** (above), introduced by the New Jersey-based company around 1962 after a collaboration with New York sessionman **Vinnie Bell** (pictured opposite). Bell and Danelectro clearly based the guitar on the traditional Greek bouzouki, apparently inspired by the music in the 1960 movie *Never On Sunday*.

The Best of
VINCENT BELL
Arranged & Produced By
CHARLES CAELELO

STEREO MS 3192

The World Is Waiting For The Sunrise
▪ Ebb Tide ▪ Just A Little Kiss ▪ Lover
▪ While We're Dancing ▪ Tea For Two ▪
Baker Street ▪ Never On Sunday ▪ Brazil
▪ Guitar Boogie ▪ Lady Of Spain ▪ Golden
Wildwood Flower ▪ How High The Moon ▪
Caravan ▪ Bye Bye Blues ▪ Carioca ▪

MUSICOR

● Rickenbacker was aware of the early electric 12-strings by Stratosphere, Gibson, and Danelectro, and decided to test its own version, making a number of **prototypes**. This one-off 1964 12-string (main guitar) has a much longer headstock than the design Rickenbacker generally used. Pictured above is the **first electric 12-string** that Rickenbacker made, one of three different experiments the company built in 1963. Its serial number indicates it was produced in July, and it is the only one of the three that has the early-style cooker knobs and gold pickguard. This test guitar went to cabaret artist **Suzi Arden** (right), whose band The Suzi Arden Show was kitted out with Rick gear. (The original flat "trapeze" tailpiece has been replaced with a later "R" type.)

47

already distributed Fender there; and Selmer, Gibson's agent in the UK. Like many of his countrymen, Roy Morris of Rose-Morris was aware of the growing popularity of The Beatles in Britain, and he included a clipping of a magazine picture of the group with the letter he sent to Rickenbacker in November. "This shows the Rickenbackers used by the group I mentioned to you," he wrote to Hall.

The following month, Morris and his colleague Maurice Woolf visited Hall in Santa Ana and clinched the UK distribution deal. They made an initial order of 450 pieces, consisting of solid model 615, hollow models 325, 335, and 345, and a bass.

Then came the crucial moment. Woolf offered a tip for Hall in a letter he sent to California in December. "We think it would be an excellent idea if you, as the manufacturer of Rickenbacker Guitars, were to contact The Beatles' manager and offer them a certain amount of American publicity on their forthcoming visit to the States." He then gave Brian Epstein's address in Liverpool, explaining that Epstein was The Beatles' manager "and is, I believe, a very charming fellow. It is impossible to exaggerate [The Beatles'] influence at the present moment in this country. We will be getting in touch with him eventually but an initial letter from you could be very important for us all".

Hall said later that he heard about The Beatles through one of his salesmen, possibly Harold Buckner. "He told me that on one of their recordings they used a Rickenbacker guitar – you could tell from the sound. When I heard they were coming to the United States, I called Epstein and made a date to meet with them in New York."[28]

Hall phoned Epstein early in January 1964 and arranged a meeting for the following month, when the group were due to set foot in the United States for the first time. He wrote to confirm the meeting, telling Epstein he would have amps, echo units, "and some other new products by Rickenbacker available for the boys to try out while they are here in New York". Perhaps the mention of those "new products" means that Hall already thought that the company's brand new electric 12-string might be good to include in the selection he intended to show The Beatles during the upcoming meeting.

Hall was used to encouraging well-known players to use Rickenbacker merchandise. He'd arranged deals in recent years with stars such as Rick Nelson and Jim Reeves. But he was becoming aware that further use of Rickenbacker products by The Beatles would assume far greater importance. "I have a definite date to talk to The Beatles in New York," he wrote to salesman Harold Buckner in late January. "However *please* do not mention this to a soul as I do not want our competition to know I will be there in New York while they are there." Hall added a PS: "The Beatles now have the Number 1 single record in the United States and the Number 3 bestselling album."

Rickenbacker set up a special display at the Savoy Hilton hotel in New York City and had guitarist and harmonica player Jean 'Toots' Thielemans on hand in case any demonstrations were necessary. On February 8, The Beatles were due to come over and take a look at the guitars and equipment. Unfortunately, George Harrison was unwell and stayed in bed back at the Plaza Hotel.

Rickenbackers were not new to Harrison. He was familiar with Lennon's model 325, of course, which Lennon had acquired back in 1960 during one of the group's residencies in Hamburg, Germany. But briefly, in summer 1963, Harrison used a Rickenbacker model 425, which he'd bought when he and his brother visited their sister in the US. (His 425 was without vibrato – which was how this model appeared until 1965.) He soon tired of his new Rick and returned to his accustomed Gretsch Country Gentleman guitar. But it was these two guitars – Lennon with his 325, Harrison with 425 – that appeared in the clipping that Morris had sent to Hall.

Hall remembered the arrival of the three fit Beatles at the Rickenbacker display at the New York hotel. "They came over to our suite, and we showed them the new 12-string we'd just developed." Hall had brought from California the second of the company's trio of experimental electric 12-string guitars. It had 'deluxe' features like a model 360 six-string. "John Lennon wanted to know if he could take it back and show it to George Harrison. He asked me if I would go with them back to their suite, so we carried it across the park there in New York."[29]

Harrison evidently enjoyed the new 12-string. "Straight away I liked that you knew exactly which string was which," he recalled later. "Some 12-strings … you're turning the wrong [tuner] there's so many of them."[30] Hall described the scene. "George was playing [the 12-string] and the telephone rang, and John Lennon went to answer it in another room. He came back pretty soon, and he said some radio station wanted to talk to George Harrison because they'd heard he was ill. Pretty soon I heard George telling them about the instrument that John Lennon had brought over for him to look at, over the air. They said do you like that instrument? And George said: I sure do! They said well, if we buy it for you, will you play it? And he said yes."[31]

Rickenbacker promised to provide a few more instruments for its new Liverpudlian friends. It would send to Lennon a black 325 model, with the company's new five-control layout, to replace his road-weary early-style 325. Hall also promised to send Lennon a special one-off 12-string version in the 325 style, and manager Brian Epstein requested that Rickenbacker make a second 360-style 12-string guitar for another of his famous clients, Gerry Marsden of Gerry & The Pacemakers.

For the two *Ed Sullivan* appearances in New York on February 9 (one went out on live TV, the other was taped for later broadcast) Lennon used his old 325. But for The Beatles' second live Sullivan appearance, broadcast seven days later from the Deauville Hotel in Miami, Florida, Lennon gave the newly arrived five-knob 325 its public debut. Famously, the two live shows were overwhelmingly popular, each with an audience of some 70 million viewers. No doubt F.C. Hall allowed himself a smile as he watched the group perform in CBS's New York studio.

After their thoroughly successful invasion of the United States, The Beatles returned to Britain and to EMI's Abbey Road studio in north London to finish recording their next single, 'Can't Buy Me Love'. It was February 25 1964, and Harrison celebrated his 21st

● Rickenbacker was alerted to **The Beatles'** use of their guitars by **Roy Morris** at Rose-Morris (letter, left) and by Rickenbacker salesman **Harold Buckner** (top left).

● Rickenbacker made this **second electric 12-string** in December 1963, and photographed it then at the factory (above left). Just two months later, a lucky **George Harrison** was given this historic 360/12 during his group's first US visit. He used it subsequently on many great Beatle records and concerts.

● As with many bands in the 60s, there were a variety of reasons why The Beatles ended up with the guitars they used – including budget, luck, and aspiration. They certainly craved American guitars – that's what their heroes used – and a mix of luck and aspiration brought them some Rickenbackers. **John Lennon** was the first, buying a model 325 in Hamburg, and **George Harrison** briefly played a **425** (above, far right). During the group's US visit early in 1964, Rick boss Francis Hall hosted a gear demo for them (see hotel message, below). George got a **360/12** (main guitar) and John a new version of his **325**, with which he is pictured (opposite) at a radio session.

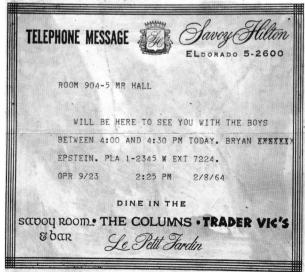

birthday by giving the new Rickenbacker 12-string its first recorded outing, on the B-side, 'You Can't Do That' (and Lennon used his new 325, too). When the single was released just under a month later, guitarists stopped in their tracks as they heard the opening seconds of 'You Can't Do That'. What on earth was that instrument playing the simple blues riff at the start? Was it a harpsichord? Some electric keyboard? Surely not a guitar?

Harrison himself was aware of the ambiguity, telling curious interviewers in 1964: "It's a great guitar, you can get so many different sounds from it – it's like experimenting with an organ,"[32] and: "It sounds a bit like an electric piano, I always think, but you can get a nice fat sound out of it."[33] *Melody Maker*, the British pop newspaper read by musicians, called the electric 12-string "the beat boys' secret weapon – it could become *the* musical instrument of 1964".[34]

In fact, Harrison's Rickenbacker wasn't the first electric 12-string on a British recording session. That honour belongs to a Burns guitar played by Hank Marvin of The Shadows. Marvin, a Fender Stratocaster player, had teamed up with British guitar-maker Jim Burns to design a new solidbody six-string electric. Burns also came up with an electric 12-string, and around October 1963 Marvin received an early sample of the Burns Double Six. He took it along to various sessions at EMI's Abbey Road studios in London where he was recording with Cliff Richard & The Shadows.

Marvin had intended to record 'Don't Talk To Him' using the Burns 12, but problems arose, so instead he doubled a six-string line to achieve the prominent hookline. A few weeks later, however, he recorded another Cliff session and played the prototype Burns 12-string for 'On The Beach'. Unusually, the 12 was strung like a six-string bass plus octave strings, clearly heard on the song's low-down double-string runs. Later in November, Marvin used the Burns 12 with regular stringing for 'I'm The Lonely One'. These Cliff Richard songs weren't released until 1964 – in the UK singles chart, 'I'm The Lonely One' went to Number 8 in February and 'On The Beach' to 7 in July – but they are important as early British recordings of the electric 12-string sound.

The very first release of a British record with electric 12-string – just ahead of The Beatles and well ahead of Cliff & The Shads – was the result of another Abbey Road session. Paul McCartney gave one of his songs to Peter & Gordon, a new duo signed to EMI. They recorded their single 'A World Without Love' at Abbey Road in January 1964, with sessionman Vic Flick on guitar.

Flick had been a member of The John Barry Seven and is best known now for his guitar lead on the James Bond theme. On the Peter & Gordon record, Flick plays the powerful opening five-note guitar line on a Vox Bouzouki electric 12-string. He adds some more flurries during and after the organ solo, and closes the record with another strong series of 12-string lines. The single was released in late February 1964 and made Number 1 on both sides of the Atlantic, bringing the electric 12 sound to the attention of many listeners.

Vox is renowned today for its amplifiers, but from the early 60s the British company also made and marketed guitars. Vox's first two electric 12-string models were the

Bouzouki and the Phantom XII, probably issued late in 1963 or early in '64. Flick's Bouzouki model, despite the name, had a very Fender-like solid body, three pickups, and, remarkably for a 12-string, a vibrato system.

"The Macari's shop in London gave me the guitar as a promo. It was terrible to play," Flick recalls. "Vox had sent it to Macari's for Hank Marvin, as they had done a deal with him, but I believe he didn't want the 12-string. I was in the shop one day, and Macari gave it to me. I think Hank was using another 12-string, and the producer of Peter & Gordon, Norman Newell, had heard the sound and asked me to bring one to the session. At that time, The Shadows and Peter & Gordon both recorded at EMI."[35]

Meanwhile, from February to June 1964, The Beatles worked in the studio and in front of the cameras to complete their *Hard Day's Night* movie and soundtrack album, and both were released in July. Harrison's Rick 12-string makes an impressive mark, sonically and visually. Its most famous appearance is for the striking opening chord of the title song, 'A Hard Day's Night', ringing out with the distinctive overtones and harmonic complexity that immediately set apart the sound of a prominent electric 12.

That complexity has turned the 'Hard Day's Night' chord into an unsolvable puzzle for musicians. Producer George Martin explains its strategic importance: "We knew [the song] would open both the film and the soundtrack LP, so we wanted a particularly strong and effective beginning. The strident guitar chord was the perfect launch."[36] Certainly Harrison's new Rickenbacker 12-string provides the chord's distinct flavour, but that's not the only ingredient. It's quite an earful: also in there is a chord from Lennon on his acoustic-with-pickup Gibson J-160E, McCartney adding a single note on his Hofner bass, and George Martin playing a piano chord.

The central solo section of 'A Hard Day's Night' is another sonic mind-bender. From bootlegs of the session tapes, it's clear that Harrison knew what he wanted to do in the solo right from Take 1, but despite his bandmates' amusement at his inability to nail it straight away, he decided after Take 3 to simply leave rhythm guitar in the solo bars and then slot in the lead on a later overdub. George Martin's solution was to slow the tape and record himself on piano and Harrison on Rick 12, playing the solo an octave down.

Engineer Geoff Emerick observed the process. "I was told to roll the tape at half speed while George [Martin] went down into the studio and doubled the guitar solo on an out-of-tune upright piano. Both parts had to be played simultaneously because there was only one free track, and it was fascinating watching the two Georges – Harrison and Martin – working side by side in the studio, foreheads furrowed in concentration as they played the rhythmically complex solo in tight unison on their respective instruments."[37]

Three more highlights for Harrison's new toy on the *Hard Day's Night* album underline how important this new guitar and its gorgeous new sound were to the Beatle guitarist. Our guide here is Andre Barreau, a musician who since 1979 has played the George Harrison part in The Bootleg Beatles. His first choice is 'I Should Have Known Better' with its beautiful 12-string solo. "And that lovely end 6th chord," says Barreau. "It's a brilliant

● British guitarists of the 60s took to the sound of electric 12-string with enthusiasm, and the UK's guitar-makers did their best to fuel the demand. The first 12-string to turn up at an important recording session was a Burns played by Hank Marvin, of The Shadows, on some Cliff Richard records cut in late 1963. Burns was bought in 1965 by the US Baldwin company, which produced its own versions of many Burns models, including this 1965 **Baldwin Double Six** (main guitar). The other big British brand at the time was Vox, which made an early electric 12, the **Bouzouki** (catalogue, right), around the start of 1964. Sessionman Vic Flick used one on Peter & Gordon's hit 'World Without Love'. Vox made other 12s, including this

"BOUZOUKI"

A twelve string electric guitar constructed of solid lightweight hardwood, contoured body finished in high lustre polyester. Choice of colours. Natural polished sycamore neck, with inset adjustable truss rod. Fitted with high grade single pole pick-ups and precision arranged electronic circuitry to provide maximum range of tone control.
The six pairs of strings are tunable in accordance with requirements.

● A visitor to the Rickenbacker HQ plays the company's **Astro Kit** guitar (right) in 1964. It was sold as a kit of parts that was designed to be built into this very un-Rickenbacker and futuristic electric instrument.

● **George Harrison** (above) used his new **Rickenbacker 360/12** as soon as he was back in the UK after getting the guitar on his group's US visit in February 1964. The job in hand was the *Hard Day's* *Night* movie and soundtrack album, and he used his new toy extensively. The scene above shows the group filming a sequence for the song 'If I Fell' in the movie, with George strumming that big 12-string sound. Many other musicians took note.

piece of playing, and so simple. I remember it from when I went to see the film, as a young boy, at the Morden Odeon in 1964. I remember clearly seeing George playing that guitar. I don't think I knew it was a 12-string, back then, but I knew it was different." He was not alone in his curiosity.

Next up is 'I'm Happy Just To Dance With You', a Lennon song written for Harrison to sing. "The good thing about this from a guitarist's point of view," says Barreau, "is that George is playing that opening chord, the C sharp minor, with two Es in it, so you have tons of Es chiming away on the 12-string – quite beautifully."

Last in our trio of *Hard Day's Night* Rickenbacker moments is 'Any Time At All,' full of 12-string themes and decorative lines as well as a bewildering solo constructed from tape-speed-altered piano and 12-string, using a similar technique to the title track's carefully assembled solo-section montage. "That method had begun back on 'Not A Second Time' on the 1963 album *With The Beatles*, where George Martin added the low piano," explains Barreau. "It was the start of them putting piano and guitar together – and 'Any Time At All' is a great example of how with the new 12-string sound they developed that idea into something special on *Hard Day's Night*."[38]

During 1963 and 1964, Martin had certainly been developing the idea of combining guitars and pianos for interesting sounds. Sometimes the guitarist alone provides the sound – as with a further example from *With The Beatles*, 'I Wanna Be Your Man', where the chorus guitar hook sounds like a detuned and a regular six-string playing 12-string-like octave runs.

For Billy J Kramer & The Dakotas' single 'Little Children', which made Number 1 in the UK during February 1964, the big riff consists of stacked-up pianos and guitars. Dakotas guitarist Mike Maxfield recalls the Abbey Road session well. "I overdubbed the guitar in unison and then played it again an octave higher, and then our producer George Martin added the piano."

Earlier, during 1963, Martin used a technique while recording another hit with Maxfield, 'The Cruel Sea', an instrumental by The Dakotas. Maxfield points out that he has never owned a 12-string guitar, Rickenbacker or otherwise, despite what many people assume when they hear this record. "In fact, I used a six-string Guild Starfire. I played in octaves, using a pick and my third finger, and it was slightly detuned and overdubbed to produce the 12-string-like sound. I think it was engineer Norman Smith who suggested the detune. George Martin was very pleased with the finished recording."[39]

Back with The Beatles, Harrison and Lennon began to use their new Rickenbackers on stage as well as in the studio. In summer 1964, the group returned to the US for more concerts, playing the Hollywood Bowl in Los Angeles on August 23, where Rickenbacker's F.C. Hall and his son John were in the audience. They must have been delighted to see George Harrison and John Lennon step on stage carrying the 12-string and the 325 and use them to launch into the opening song, 'Twist And Shout'.

Lennon had by now received his one-off 320-style 12-string, but he didn't use it much.

This is hardly surprising, given the problems of tuning and playability that would come with 12 strings on such a slim short-scale neck. Harrison, however, continued to play his Rick 12 in the studio – listen to how he uses it throughout the sublime 'Every Little Thing' and for the strong riff of 'What You're Doing' from *Beatles For Sale*, or that sparkling intro to the 'Ticket to Ride' single.

During The Beatles' third US tour, in 1965, Harrison was given a new Rickenbacker 12-string, a 360/12 in the company's new 'rounded'-body style. It was this instrument rather than his first 12 that he used to record 'If I Needed Someone' for the *Rubber Soul* album, capo'd at the seventh fret for a very Byrds-like sound. And that was the last Beatles track with electric 12. Harrison stuck solely to six-strings through the last years of the group's career, although he would return to the 12 later and maintained fond memories for his Rickenbacker (you can hear it prominently on 'Fish On The Sand' on his 1987 solo album *Cloud Nine*). "That sound," he said later, "you just associate with those early 60s Beatle records. The Rickenbacker 12-string sound is a sound on its own."[40]

The Beatles movie *A Hard Day's Night* in particular and the group's subsequent success in general had a remarkable effect, inspiring many youngsters to get an electric guitar and form a pop group. It looked like so much fun. And with Rickenbackers so prominent in that film, the company benefited enormously. F.C.'s son John Hall says, "The Beatles gave the company a kind of visibility and unpaid-for advertising that we couldn't possibly have garnered any other way."[41]

Rickenbacker added a large third building to its factory in Santa Ana to cope with the new demand. As F.C. Hall recalled in wonderfully understated fashion: "There were musicians who wanted to make the same sound as The Beatles had, so they started purchasing Rickenbackers too."[42]

In Britain, this coincided with the new availability of Rickenbackers through Rose-Morris, the distribution firm run by Roy Morris and Maurice Woolf who had tipped off Rickenbacker about The Beatles in the first place.

Morris, from his base in London, wrote to F.C. Hall in California late in 1963, enquiring about the guitars that the British company were about to start selling in the UK. "I understand that models 325, 335, and 345 will all be manufactured with the same 'traditional' f-holes which we saw on the 325 you had in your showroom, and that all instruments will be manufactured in your 'fireglo' finish," Morris wrote.

For a number of years, Rickenbacker had produced some of the short-scale 300-series guitars with an f-hole, distinct from others that had an unbroken top. Morris and Woolf evidently took a liking to the f-hole and asked for it to be used on the bigger-body guitars, too, instead of Rickenbacker's standard slash-shape soundhole. Most of the semi-hollow guitars that Rickenbacker subsequently made for export had f-holes. These export guitars – which went to Canada, Australia, and Italy, as well as to the UK – also used Rickenbacker's earlier style of plain black control knobs with a half-line marker on the top.

Rickenbacker sold some guitars with f-holes in the US, too, referring to them with an

● The Kim Sisters were a Korean girl-group who went from entertaining US troops at home to big success on the Ed Sullivan TV show in the US. **Sook-ja Kim** (above) is pictured in 1960 playing a Rickenbacker **320**, this one with the f-hole that some Ricks featured.

● Rickenbacker gave this **320/12** to John Lennon in 1964. It's an unwieldy combination of the small 325 Lennon knew, but with 12 strings, and was little used. Future Rick boss **John Hall** was pictured (top left) with the Lennon guitar before it shipped.

● On The Beatles' final tour in 1966, **George Harrison** played the new-style **360/12** that Rickenbacker had given him the previous year. He played it (above) on 'If I Needed Someone'. The song appeared on the *Rubber Soul* album, marking the last appearance of an electric 12-string on a Beatles record. Rickenbacker meanwhile applied the 12-string idea to another body shape, for the **450/12** (right) of 1965.

S (for Special) suffix – for example a 345S. Rickenbacker's Dick Burke recalls that the f-hole made little difference to the production process. "It was the same instrument except for the f-hole, using the same jig. It was a simple job to change to the f-hole – it just meant changing a few screws on the jig and putting in a new pattern."[43]

Rose-Morris received its first deliveries of Rickenbackers probably around March 1964, and the company adopted its own stock numbers to identify the models. Rose-Morris imported a lot of guitars and other musical equipment, resulting in a large catalogue, and used four-digit stock numbers to identify the various products. Model 1846, for example, was an Eko hollowbody electric from Italy; model 1970 a Top Twenty solidbody electric from Japan; and model 1998 a Rickenbacker 345S semi-hollow electric from California. These reference numbers were for internal use: they did not appear on the guitars and had nothing to do with Rickenbacker.

Rose-Morris catalogued its first Rickenbacker models, all non-deluxe vibrato-equipped models, as follows: 1998 (a 345S) priced at £178/10/-; 1997 (335S) at £166/19/-; 1996 (325S) at £166/19/-; and 1995 (615S) at £141/15/-. (British currency in the 60s was written in the form £/s/d – pounds, shillings, and pence. There were twelve pence in a shilling and twenty shillings in a pound.)

Soon, the Rose-Morris line had an addition. Morris sat down to write to Hall in March 1964. "I have now been informed that the instruments which you provided during The Beatles' recent visit to the States were a model 325 for John Lennon and, to my considerable surprise, a 12-string instrument for George Harrison," said Morris. "I was not even aware that you made such an instrument, and obviously it will be necessary for me to have full details immediately; there can be little doubt that we will receive some demand for this instrument."

This rather bad-tempered letter resulted in Rose-Morris adding a 12-string to its imported line of Rickenbackers. A sample was dispatched at the start of June, and the first shipment of 25 not too long after that. This export 12-string model had a bound body with flat top, like Harrison's guitar, but featured dot position-markers on the fingerboard and an f-hole where Harrison's had triangle markers and a regular slash soundhole. Rose-Morris catalogued it as model 1993 – to Rickenbacker it was a 330S/12 – and priced the instrument at £222/10/-.

Rickenbacker added two electric 12-string models to its own domestic US line during 1964. The 360/12 was a 12-string 360 (two pickups, double-bound body, 'slash' soundhole, triangle fingerboard markers) and first appeared on the July 1964 pricelist at $550. The 370/12 (a three-pickup version of the 360/12) also launched in 1964, although it did not appear on a pricelist at the time and was probably a special-order item.

Also in 1964, Rickenbacker introduced a new-style body for the 'deluxe' models – 360, 360/12, 365, 370, 370/12, and 375 – with a less pointed and more rounded look to the front of the body. There was sometimes binding on the slash soundhole, while the curved body front meant that body binding was now confined to the back edge.

The revised body was designed to be more comfortable for the player, and while Rickenbacker used the new streamlined look as its main production style from 1964 for the models noted, old-style versions ('sharp' body edges, bound front and back) remained available on special order. (Later, old-style models would be identified on Rickenbacker model lists with OS or WB model names.)

Rickenbacker's press release described the new design as having "rounded edges" and "contoured shaping" and added: "The smooth roundness avoids all that is harsh and yields flowing lines for smooth, easy playing – and handling."

The new style did not require big changes at the factory and was simply a cosmetic alteration: the old-style 'sharp edge' and the new-style 'round edge' could be produced from the same body blank. "Everything was the same," reports Dick Burke. "For the rounded style, we just shaped the top of it instead of putting in the binding groove and adding the binding."

Rickenbacker made a further change in the early 60s by redesigning the tailpiece. Previously, this had been a rather plain trapeze-shape piece of flat metal. During 1963, Rickenbacker introduced a striking new tailpiece in the shape of a large 'R'. Dick Burke explains its origins. "We copied that from the Washington Redskins football team – they had a similar 'R' for Redskins on their hat. Mr Hall wanted a new tailpiece, and obviously 'R' went with Rickenbacker. I remembered seeing those Redskins hats and that the way the tail of the 'R' came up looked good, so we just copied it from there."

Two further 12-string models appeared on Rickenbacker's US pricelist for August 1965. The 450/12 was a 12-string 450 (solidbody with two pickups) at $294.50; the 330/12 was the 'non-deluxe' version of the 360/12, with dot fingerboard markers and unbound body, at $444.50.

In contrast to those important instruments, Rickenbacker produced a neat little build-it-yourself solidbody electric guitar kit aimed at the Christmas 1964 gift market. The Astro Kit guitar, designed by Marvin Boyd, came as a box of 25 parts, including unpainted body and neck. "It will be educational," claimed the instructions, "and lots of fun to assemble." Also, helpfully: "If you are not familiar with wood finishes you should contact your favorite paint store for helpful hints." It's not difficult to picture the cosy Christmas scene as a paint-streaked Astro Kit recipient finally proceeded to Step 13 in the instructions: "Stick plate to top side of head."

British beat-group guitarists lined up during 1964 and into 1965 for an opportunity to join the electric 12-string club, and some opted for Rose-Morris's newly-available model 1993. The Searchers stand out now as an important group in the unfolding story. The jangling intro of 'Needles And Pins', a big UK hit in January 1964, sounds like a significant example of early electric 12-string. In fact, it is once again the sound of doubled six-string guitars, achieved in a similar way to the experiments at Abbey Road.

Tony Hatch, the group's producer at Pye Records, explains how they did it. "By 1963, when I first recorded The Searchers, the Ampex three-track tape recorder had been

● British importer **Rose-Morris** began selling Rickenbackers in the UK in 1964, and these two first-year examples of the 12-string model, which Rose- Morris called the **1993**, show the distinctive features, including a trapeze tailpiece at first, then an "R", the f-hole on the body, and black control knobs.

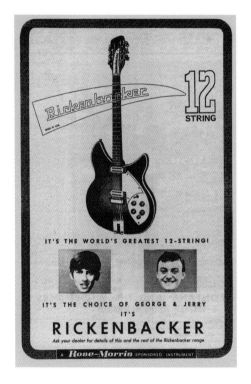

● **Rose-Morris** sold and promoted Rickenbacker export models in the UK from 1964, issuing an attractive **catalogue** (top) that featured a full page on the 12-string (left) and the other models across a colourful spread (centre). Their ads were effective, too, and naturally enough drew upon the most famous players then using Rickenbacker guitars. It was no exaggeration for the company to say: "Rickenbacker: the Beatle Backer." **John Lennon** (above right) was pictured alongside the Rose-Morris equivalent of his favoured 325, which the UK firm called model 1996. When it came to the 12-string – Rose-Morris's model 1993 – the British firm boasted (right) that "the world's greatest 12-string" was the instrument chosen by **Gerry Marsden** (not Jerry) of Gerry & The Pacemakers, as well as **George Harrison**.

● Rickenbacker gave its "deluxe" models a new look in 1964, as this 1965 **360/12** demonstrates, notably a "rounded" body front without binding. Earlier in '64, at a trade show, guitarist **Danny DeLacy** (opposite) demo'd an experimental early 360/12, similar to George Harrison's original guitar but with an f-hole.

63

superseded by the four-track. The group's early singles, 'Sweets For My Sweet' and 'Sugar And Spice', were recorded live – vocals and instruments – direct to the four-track, and then we mixed them to a two-track.

"By late 1963, Pye had acquired a second four-track, and the two were placed side by side in Studio 1's control room. At that time, the two four-track machines couldn't be electronically synchronised, although my principal balance engineer, Ray Prickett, could often get them running in sync for anything up to a minute – which was handy if we wanted to lift part of a vocal from the second machine and put it back on the first.

"So from 'Needles And Pins' onwards," says Hatch, "we had the flexibility of being able to record instrument tracks on the first four-track and then mix and copy them to the second machine, adding instrument overdubs [such as the second guitar] and/or vocals at the time or later. I'm not saying we did this all the time – it all depended on the song and how we wanted to handle it."[44]

A few singles down the line, and 'Someday We're Gonna Love Again' failed to make the Top 10 after a run of three Number 1s and a Number 2. Searchers guitarist Mike Pender recalls: "Drummer Chris Curtis and I wondered what we were going to do. We were a little bit concerned, so we said we have to get a great song for the next one." The group had already successfully covered 'Needles And Pins', as originally recorded by Jackie DeShannon, so they pounced on her latest, 'When You Walk In The Room'. It was DeShannon's own song and was a minor hit for the singer in the US at the end of 1963.

DeShannon recalls writing the song's main riff on guitar but says that Glen Campbell played the distinctive 12-string line on the session. "It was really funny. I had such nerves. Glen could have played it perfectly, but I didn't want that. I wanted it more raunchy and funky, like I played it. Glen thought people were going to think he played badly. I kept saying, 'Well, never mind,' because I'm not a great musician by any means. It was a very different approach in those days."[45]

Pender says they listened to the DeShannon version with great interest. "It was pretty light. I said to Chris, that riff there, it starts and it's in between the first couple of lines – that's really got to stand out, it's got to be important. It's not going to sound good on a six-string, no matter if we double-track it or whatever."

In July 1964, The Searchers found themselves once again on the British TV chart show *Top Of The Pops*. "We're in the dressing room with the telly on," says Pender, "and all the songs from last week's chart are playing. The Beatles come on, it's 'Hard Day's Night', and there's Harrison with this amazing guitar. I'd seen Rickenbackers before, but I said to Chris, listen to that – that's the sound we want for 'When You Walk In The Room'. The rest is history, really."[46]

When Pender got back to Liverpool, he bought a Rickenbacker Rose-Morris model 1993 12-string from Crane's music store and used it on the recording session for 'When You Walk In The Room', probably also in July. The Searchers took the general idea of DeShannon's record and strengthened the 12-string line, making it central to the sound of the single. Their cover went to Number 3 in Britain in September 1964 and into the US Top 40 a few months later. A certain group forming in California was among those who heard and noted its special sound.

The Searchers were given a set of English-made Burns electrics around this time, too. Among them was the Double Six electric 12, and Pender says he used it on some recordings, as well as television shows and concerts. On an interesting TV appearance for the December 1964 single 'What Have They Done To The Rain', Pender and second guitarist John McNally each played a Double Six – McNally's finished in green and Pender's in white.

American guitarists were drawn to electric 12s too, and specifically the Rickenbacker 12, following the impact of The Beatles. One such musician was Jim (later Roger) McGuinn, in California, whose group The Jet Set was about to change its name to The Byrds. McGuinn already had a lot of experience with acoustic 12-string guitars, at first a Stella and then a Gibson. "When The Byrds were getting together," he says, "I played a Gibson 12-string acoustic guitar that Bobby Darin had given me after he accidentally destroyed the one I was using to back him up in his stage show.

"The Byrds were heavily influenced by The Beatles," McGuinn explains. "I started using a magnetic pickup in my Gibson to approximate The Beatles' sound, but it wasn't quite the same one we were hearing on their records."

Then came *A Hard Day's Night*, which opened in movie theatres across the US in August 1964. It offered McGuinn and friends the chance to get a closer look at the Beatle hardware. "One night, we all went down to the Pix theatre in Hollywood to see *A Hard Day's Night*," says McGuinn. "We carefully noted the brands and models of their instruments. John had a little black 325 Rickenbacker, Paul had a Hofner bass, Ringo played Ludwig drums, and George had a Gretsch six-string and a Rickenbacker that looked like a six-string – until he turned sideways. The camera revealed another six strings hidden in the back. I knew right then the secret of their wonderful guitar sound. It was a Rickenbacker 12-string!"

That crucial sideways view of George's guitar comes during the first song the group perform, about 13 minutes into the movie, as they mime to 'I Should Have Known Better' in the mail-van on a train. The camera offers perfect, if fleeting, views of the Rickenbacker's unusual two-tier tuning pegs. More clues come later as the group fool around on a TV set with 'If I Fell'. Of course, McGuinn and all the other fascinated guitarists who studied the Beatle movie had no freeze-frame DVDs or clips on YouTube. Instead, they had to make multiple visits to the cinema. And it was clear to the eagle-eyed Byrd, and others, that this was no regular six-string electric.

Later, the group's manager arranged for an investor to loan The Byrds $5,000 to buy new instruments. "We went down to the local music shop," says McGuinn, "and bought a Rickenbacker 360/12, along with a Gretsch six-string and a set of Ludwig drums. The new instruments gave us a sense of confidence that we hadn't had up to that point."

McGuinn's first Rickenbacker – we'll call it Number 1 – was a stock new-style 360/12, in other words with rounded body-front. It was made by Rickenbacker in October 1964, and he probably got it the following month, when The Byrds signed their deal with Columbia Records. The guitar had Rickenbacker's mapleglo finish (natural) and the regular layout of two pickups alongside five controls and a selector switch. It was this 12-string that he used through The Byrds' first year of gigs and recordings, and it's all over the classic 1965 albums *Mr. Tambourine Man* and *Turn! Turn! Turn!*.

"The Rickenbacker 12-string with the aid of electronic compression in the studio gave us the distinctive 'jingle jangle' sound that we would later be known for," says McGuinn.[47] The compression he refers to is a studio effect designed to control and contain the sound of recorded music. At first, compressors were used to limit the potentially wide dynamic range of a recording to match the limitations of existing recording media. Soon, compressors were used as an effect, exploiting the way they could make loud sounds quieter and quiet sounds louder, providing a result that sounded smoother and with longer sustain.

"The Rick by itself is kind of thuddy," explains McGuinn. "It doesn't ring. But if you add a compressor, you get that long sustain. To be honest, I found this by accident. The [Columbia studio] engineer Ray Gerhardt would run compressors on everything to protect his precious equipment from loud rock'n'roll. He compressed the heck out of my 12-string … that's how I got my jingle-jangle tone. It's really squashed down, but it jumps out from the radio."[48]

McGuinn used his 360/12 to good effect on The Byrds' very first single. He recorded 'Mr Tambourine Man' at Columbia's Hollywood studio in January 1965, along with session players for this debut session, and it was released in April. Bob Dylan's lyrics even included that most perfect (and now most clichéd) description of the Rickenbacker 12-string sound: "jingle jangle". As 'Tambourine Man' topped the charts, guitarists hearing the four-bar intro, dominated by McGuinn's chiming Rickenbacker, wondered what kind of instrument could possibly make this striking sound.

In February 1966, McGuinn modified his 'Number 1' 360/12. He asked Rickenbacker to add a third pickup, giving the look of a model 370, and to install new controls matching his redesigned layout. The rewired result had three knobs in a curving line (a volume each for the three pickups), one knob above (master volume), and two selectors (a three-way selecting each pickup, and a tone-option switch).

McGuinn enhanced the sound of his guitar on-stage by adding a Vox V806 Treble Booster, a small box designed to sit between guitar and amp and provide what Vox described as "super extra glass-shattering treble". McGuinn got the idea from the Jefferson Airplane guitarist Paul Kantner, another keen Rick 12-string fan. "[He] turned me on to the Vox Treble Booster in 1966," says McGuinn. "I took the Rick apart and installed it in the guitar. It really was an outboard box that gave me some gain."[49] McGuinn added a small flickswitch to turn the booster on and off, next to the selectors in the revised control layout. Unfortunately, McGuinn lost Number 1. "It was while we were performing at a college in New York," he remembers, "and I think I borrowed a fireglo 360 12-string until I could replace the first one with another 'rounded' mapleglo [model], in 1966. I also added a Vox treble booster to that one, and it became my main guitar."[50]

McGuinn's guitar in fireglo – Rickenbacker's name for its red finish – seems to have been a brief stopgap, a 360/12 with regular features that he got in early '66. In June that year, he acquired what we'll call Number 2, a new mapleglo Rick three-pickup 370/12 that replaced Number 1. Again he called for his special custom control layout, which Rickenbacker duly supplied. He used Number 2 from then until early 1971, playing it on a further sequence of great recordings and concerts.

He replaced that presumably worn-out guitar with another custom-wired 370/12, Number 3, which Rickenbacker made for him in June 1970. "Rickenbacker generously gave us a 50 percent discount on all guitars," says McGuinn. He also acquired a 1970 12-string 'lightshow' guitar with slanted frets, model 341/12SF, and a few years later a model 362/12, which was a six-and-12-string double-neck.

The Byrds had a Fender electric 12-string, too, the solidbody Electric XII model, which McGuinn says he used occasionally in the studio. Gene Clark is seen playing the Fender during one of the group's early TV performances of 'Mr Tambourine Man', with McGuinn using his Rick 12 alongside. How odd for the group's tambourine man to play guitar on this of all songs – or maybe that was the joke?

There are many sparkling highlights among McGuinn's recordings with The Byrds, and the group's remarkable run of singles and albums had a profound effect on many players who heard them. Rickenbacker's sales soared as guitarists tried to emulate the 12-string Byrds jangle. Absorbed with the sound, they might at first have missed McGuinn's distinctive playing style.

In his early years, when he played solely acoustic 12-string, McGuinn learned to play 5-string banjo. "Somehow, I combined the two picking styles on the [electric] 12-string. That's what makes my style sound different: it's a 5-string technique incorporated with standard guitar fingerpicking."[51]

McGuinn used a thumbpick (later a regular flatpick or plectrum between thumb and forefinger) and two fingerpicks. He combined into one fluid motion a rolling banjo technique with the fingerpicks plus lower-string picking with the flatpick. "I guess that's my sound: banjo picking, compression, and some other little folk techniques I picked up along the way."[52]

Later, as The Byrds shifted from folk-rock to psychedelia to country-rock, the 12-string became less prominent in their sound. But the distinctive chime of McGuinn's electric 12 is right there at the heart of the first four albums. If you've never heard that classic original quartet of records – and presumably that is just possible – then you might want to start with something like 'The Bells Of Rhymney' from the debut LP, Mr Tambourine Man, released in June 1965. It features a mini-orchestra of oriental-sounding electric 12-strings, but when McGuinn reaches the concise solo, he momentarily lifts his trebly Rick above the drone. Solo over, he settles back down again. It's a study in his impressive ability to construct a perfectly contained mood with the aid of his electric 12-string guitar.

Then there's the group's impressive third single, of October 1965. It features the title track from *Turn! Turn! Turn!*, another jangling celebration that peaks with a twin-12 solo as McGuinn slides around the G-string. On the B-side, 'She Don't Care About Time' (inexplicably left off the album), he quotes Bach in another beautifully succinct solo.

By the time of 'Eight Miles High' – on *Fifth Dimension* in July 1966 but first released as a single in March – McGuinn was comfortably exploiting the sustain that the studio compressor offered him. He builds a jagged, wayward, blues-scale solo in a way he could only have done on an electric 12-string, this time drawing inspiration from the jazz saxophonist John Coltrane. A little later, the version of 'Why' on *Younger Than Yesterday* (February 1967) shows how an overdriven Rick 12 could really power a song, as McGuinn slashes at the chords and hits a couple more stinging solos.

But you really need to investigate these Byrds records for yourself: there are gems buried deep within that are just as worthwhile as those that glint on the surface.

One British guitarist who found a distinctive voice with a Rickenbacker 12-string was Pete Townshend. He played a Rose-Morris 1993 version on The Who's first single, 'I Can't Explain', another hit recorded at Pye studios in London, in November '64. Guitarist and 12-string arrive with a bang at the intro as Townshend bravely plays those emphatic chords half-way up the neck on his Rick, where there's less chance of everything being in tune. The glorious result, including some jagged little solo flurries, announced the arrival of The Who in grand style. The single went to Number 8 in the UK chart the following February, and once again few guitarists could have heard it without cocking a curious ear to the gorgeous sound of the electric 12-string guitar.

Townshend describes his use of the Rick 12 on that record as "a chord machine". He continues: "The 12-string is very prominent – you can hear that typical 12-stringy sound. I remember at that session Jimmy Page saying to me oh, you've got one of those Rickenbacker 12-strings: is it true that it really sounds like a piano? And I said well, have a go at it. And he played it, and he said, 'Doesn't sound like a piano.' And I said, 'But it does have a wonderful sound.' I don't think he ever got attached to it."

Another 12-string highlight for Townshend came with his crystal-clear arpeggios that open 'A Legal Matter' on the group's first album, *My Generation*, the clarity assisted by producer Shel Talmy's practice of miking the strings of the Rickenbacker like an acoustic in addition to the amp sound. Townshend played a number of Rickenbackers with The Who until 1967, including six-string models (and he played a Fender Electric XII on various *Tommy* sessions). For some fans he became known just as much for the smashing time he had on-stage with his hapless guitars, especially Ricks. "I sometimes feel very bad about having smashed up instruments which were particularly good ones," he says, "but generally I was working with production-line instruments."[53]

Gerry Marsden's special 12-string, which his manager Brian Epstein had ordered from Rickenbacker during that meeting with The Beatles in February 1964, finally arrived later in the year. It was just like George Harrison's Rick 12, with a flat metal tailpiece, flat-top bound-front body, triangle markers, and unbound slash soundhole. There's little evidence of it on the Pacemakers records – the 12-string solo on the September 1964 hit 'It's Gonna Be All Right' sounds like an acoustic – and the Rick always looked more like an attractive prop than a serious working tool for Marsden the frontman.

Brian Jones played a Vox 12-string at times, but he also had a Rick 12 in 1965, and it's supposedly this guitar that appears somewhere in the murk of the Stones single 'Get Off Of My Cloud'. It's more evidently there on a song from the same sessions, 'Blue Turns To Grey', and later for the melodic hook of the 1966 album track 'Mother's Little Helper', which features Jones or Keith Richards on 12-string.

"That's a 12-string with a slide on it," recalls Richards, who'd had a Harmony acoustic 12-string since 1964. "It's played slightly oriental-ish. The track just needed something to make it twang. Otherwise, the song was quite vaudeville, in a way. I wanted to add some nice bite to it. And it was just one of those things where someone walked in and: look, it's an electric 12-string! It was some gashed-up job. No name on it. God knows where it came from. Or where it went. But I put it together with a bottleneck. Then we had that riff that tied the whole thing together. And I think we overdubbed onto that, because I played an acoustic guitar as well."[54]

Another great 60s band that occasionally featured the electric 12 was The Beach Boys. Jeffrey Foskett was another young budding guitarist who wanted a Rickenbacker from the moment he saw George playing one in the *Hard Day's Night* movie. In the 80s, Foskett would join The Beach Boys, at first as a replacement for guitarist Carl Wilson. But in 1974 he got his first Rick 12. Not the double-bound one like George's that he really wanted, but certainly a red one.

"I offered the guy $135 and he took it," Foskett recalls. "I scored! I had never played an instrument of that quality before. I used it every gig I played in my college career and in my early tenure with The Beach Boys. I have since retired the guitar, and it sits lovingly in my closet."

He'd seen The Beach Boys performing on the *Ed Sullivan* TV show in 1964 and noticed that Carl Wilson was using a Rickenbacker 12 for 'I Get Around'. "I thought he looked very cool playing that guitar, and it sounded great. I went to my local music shop and found a book entitled *Guitar Sounds Of The Beach Boys Featuring Carl Wilson*, and on the cover Carl was holding a Rose-Morris model 1993, the double-bound 12-string with f-hole."

Carl Wilson had acquired his 1993 model and played it live during 1964. The fact that he'd acquired it in the US means this was one of the export models sold domestically as a 330S/12. He later had a 360/12 too. Session men played electric 12 on a few Beach Boys studio cuts – Glen Campbell on 'Dance Dance Dance' and Billy Strange on 'Sloop John B' – but it was probably Wilson on 'Help Me Rhonda'.

● **Roger McGuinn** of The Byrds was one of the best-known Rickenbacker 12-string players. He got his first **360/12** at the end of 1964, and is pictured (left) with that instrument in the studio. Later he modified the guitar, adding a third pickup and altering the control layout, which is how the guitar appears today (below). For his second Rick 12-string, a three-pickup model **370/12** (above), Roger had Rickenbacker install his custom controls, including a switch for an onboard Vox treble booster. He is seen playing that guitar in late 1967 (right) and continued to use it until the early 70s, when he acquired his third Rick 12, another 370/12.

● Brits and Ricks: The Who's **Pete Townshend** (top right) poses with a number of victims in various stages of amputation; **Mike Pender** of The Searchers (right) strums a Rose-Morris 1993.

Meanwhile, the eight-year-old Jeffrey Foskett was just discovering guitars. It wasn't until he heard The Byrds a little later that it began to click. "It was only a year or so after *Hard Day's Night*, but Roger McGuinn – and his producer Terry Melcher – really brought the electric 12-string to a new level," Foskett recalls. "On the first three Byrds records, Roger's Rickenbacker overtakes you in a wash of sonic bliss. After hearing those records, I knew the difference between six strings and twelve strings. I remember asking Carl about that, and his reply was: 'Are you kidding? Nobody makes use of a Ricky like Roger.' Even he deferred to Rog in the 12-string department."

When Foskett joined The Beach Boys in the early 80s, he found out that Carl Wilson's favourite electric 12-string guitar was an Epiphone Riviera E-360TD. The head had broken off and Gibson had replaced it with a Gibson headstock. "Although Carl changed between his blond ES-335 and the Epi 12, I rarely used my six-string after that," says Foskett. "I played my Ricky 12 on every song. I took six-string solos on my 12-string Ricky and would not relinquish it for anything. Of course, I was on a quest to find an Epiphone Riviera 12 with a Gibson headstock – not knowing that only one existed."

Foskett reports that Carl Wilson loved the full sound that his Epi 12 brought to The Beach Boys on-stage. "He would use the 12 on songs that he recorded with a six-string. 'Surfer Girl' and 'God Only Knows', for example, had six-string guitar on the recordings but Carl played 12 on them on stage. I once asked him why he gave up the Ricky for live performance, and he said that he was having tuning issues with his, just like I was having with mine. Rickenbackers make you work for the glory of the sound they bring. They are temperamental, but the sound is unmatched."

Since 1999, Foskett has played with the Brian Wilson band, and when they play Beach Boys songs he draws on Carl's originals. For electric 12 he uses a blond Gibson ES-335-12 and a red Epiphone Riviera 12. "I switched to those when Brian started touring as a solo artist," he explains. "On the first tour I used a Fender Electric XII, but I needed to upgrade because the music demanded higher quality. I know that Carl played a Rickenbacker plugged directly into the board for the intro of 'California Girls', but I use the Epi on stage and it sounds extremely similar to the record. I have all my 12-strings restrung to match the Rickenbacker style of heavy string on top. F.C. Hall was a genius in stringing his 12-string that way."[55]

In the 60s, other guitar companies in the UK and the United States noticed the growing popularity of Rickenbacker's electric 12-string and began to produce their own models. One of the biggest makers was Fender, the California-based firm that introduced the first commercial solidbody electric in 1950 and the first electric bass the following year. During 1964, Fender's owners began negotiations to sell the company, and CBS completed its purchase of Fender at the very start of 1965.

A new guitar design that had been on Fender's drawing board when the CBS sale took place finally hit the music stores in the summer of 1965. The Electric XII was Fender's take on the fashion for electric 12-string guitars.

John Pisano was a jazz guitarist who earned a living playing sessions in and around Los Angeles. He'd play on movie scores and pop records and anything else the producers and arrangers wanted. Then in 1965, Herb Alpert asked Pisano to join Alpert's studio band, The Tijuana Brass, which had scored hits with 'The Lonely Bull' and a few albums. Now Alpert wanted a permanent touring band that would also record, and Pisano got the guitar job. Alpert's carrot to tempt Pisano was the opportunity to have a composition on the first album they made, *Going Places*, in 1965.

"I was doing a lot of studio work, and because of my love of jazz, I didn't feel that the music offered much to me," says Pisano. "Until I saw the royalty cheque. Don't forget, those albums sold millions. The first royalty cheque came in, and I said gee, I think this is going to be a good thing. Now I can afford to be a jazz player."

Pisano's song on the album was 'Felicia', and it features some exquisite 12-string playing on a Fender Electric XII, in marked contrast to the pop players who used their 12s in less polite surroundings. The Fender 12 remained as Pisano's main instrument for all his Tijuana Brass recordings and live dates.

"The idea was that the 12-string sound seemed to tie in with the sound of the band," he explains, referring to the quasi-Mexican 'south of the border' music that Alpert and the Tijuana Brass played. Pisano knew the guys from Fender and Gibson, and already used a Gibson acoustic 12-string. Gibson's rep told Pisano they were developing an electric 12 and promised the guitarist he would be among the first to get one. Pisano waited, but nothing showed up. Meanwhile, Fender offered the band some amplifiers. "And they brought in a 12-string. It was, from what I remember, one of half a dozen sample instruments. They wanted us to say if the instrument was satisfactory and give our take on any modifications that should be made."

After some changes to string-spacing, Pisano settled down with the Electric XII. "It had a great sound, very flexible, and it fit the music very well." A few weeks later, the Gibson man turned up with the company's new electric 12-string, the ES-335-12, and Pisano had to tell him he was too late – even though Pisano generally preferred the feel of Gibsons and Epiphones.

"But Fender treated me very well with amplifiers and guitars," says Pisano. "If we were doing a Tijuana Brass special and there was some kind of effect we needed, say a guitar in a certain colour, it would instantly be there, all finished and ready to go."

The *Going Places* album includes 'Zorba The Greek', a further recording that links the sound of the 12-string back to its Greek roots and the bouzouki. The band hit the song at a ferocious tempo on the record, and on live dates this became something of a private joke. "It was a featured number every night," Pisano recalls. "There'd be a tympani roll, all the lights would go out, and the announcer would say, 'And now ladies and gentlemen, Zorba the Greek!' Then Nick Ceroli would start this ridiculous tempo on his drums. And he'd be grinning, because he always seemed to be kicking the thing off faster and faster every night. It was like: Take this, suckers!"

● Jazz guitarist **John Pisano** joined Herb Alpert's Tijuana Brass in 1965 and began playing a **Fender Electric XII** on the band's records and concerts. Pisano had helped Fender develop its new 12-string model. He's pictured with trumpeter Alpert **in the studio** (below, second left) and in a Fender **ad** (left). Pisano's electric 12-string work is represented well on the Tijuana Brass's 1965 album **Going Places**, especially his own 'Felicia'.

● Fender's new 12-string model was the **Electric XII** (1966 example, below), first available in 1965. It was designed from the ground up as a 12-string and notable for its 12-saddle bridge, a rarity at the time.

● Carl Wilson (left) of The Beach Boys played a number of 12-string electric guitars, including Rickenbackers, and was fond of an **Epiphone Riviera** 12, similar to the 1968 example below. Wilson's had a new Gibson head fitted following an accident.

At one spectacular indoor–outdoor theatre in New York, Ceroli set up the usual breakneck tempo, and after 16 bars Pisano was due to come in with his Fender Electric XII. "Well, during the tempo set-up, a bird shit right on the fingerboard of the guitar, believe it or not. Luckily, it was someplace on the real upper register. I didn't have time to do anything – I had to start – so it just lay there and I stayed away from it. Those 16 bars were up, and I had to come in with the melody."[56]

There were no surprises in the design of the solidbody Electric XII. It had Fender's now familiar offset-waist design, just like the earlier Jazzmaster and Jaguar six-string models. The XII had a long headstock, necessary to carry the extra tuners, finishing in a distinctively curved end that earned the nickname 'hockey-stick'. An innovation was the 12-saddle bridge that allowed for precise adjustments of individual string heights and intonation, a luxury unknown on any electric 12-string so far.

The Electric XII made some further appearances on hits of the period. We've seen that The Byrds made limited use of one, but Dave Davies played a Fender on 'I'm Not Like Everybody Else', the B-side of The Kinks' summer 1966 chart single 'Sunny Afternoon', and Roy Wood bought one specifically for The Move's 1967 British Number 2 'Flowers In The Rain'. Fender's solidbody 12-string nonetheless proved a shortlived model, lasting in the company's catalogue until 1968.

In the UK, Vox made some more 12-string models following the early Bouzouki model that Vic Flick had used on Peter & Gordon's 'A World Without Love'. Flick used the same guitar for a classic electric 12-string sound on Tony Hatch's theme for the British TV soap *Crossroads*, which started broadcasting in November 1964.

Hilton Valentine, guitarist in The Animals, often used a Rose-Morris 1998 Rickenbacker six-string on stage, but he probably used a Vox electric 12-string for the big bright riffs throughout 'It's My Life', a Number 7 British hit for the group in October 1965 and a Top 30 in the US. When the group appeared on the *Ed Sullivan* show in January 1965 performing 'Don't Let Me Be Misunderstood', Valentine played a Vox Mark XII 12-string, one of the company's 'teardrop' models, a nickname drawn from the guitar's lute-like body shape.

Another British Vox 12-string user was Tony Hicks of The Hollies, who played a Phantom XII model throughout the group's September 1965 Top 5 hit 'Look Though Any Window'. Hicks also played electric 12 on a few Hollies album tracks, for example 'Tell Me To My Face' from the 1966 LP *For Certain Because*.

Rose-Morris found that demand in the UK for Rickenbackers gradually declined into 1966 and the company considered dropping model 1996 (325S). In 1967, Rose-Morris had 100 guitars back-ordered with Rickenbacker, and the British company decided to concentrate its efforts on the six-string models 1997 (335S) and 1998 (345S). They also began to investigate the possibility of importing Rickenbacker copies from an Italian manufacturer. In 1968, there was hardly any contact between Rickenbacker and Rose-Morris, and by 1969 business between the two had ceased. A company called Top Gear had started to import Rickenbackers into the UK during 1967, and Rose-Morris was bringing in Rickenbacker copies with its own Shaftesbury brand, an act hardly designed to please the Americans.

Production increased at Rickenbacker in the late 60s as US demand grew for its guitars. A note from F.C. Hall to a customer in September 1966 typifies the position. "The delivery of Rickenbacker merchandise is falling further behind each month," he wrote. "At this time I cannot quote an exact delivery date for the orders you now have on file. Nevertheless we will do our best to see that your orders are filled as soon as possible."

Six months was not an unusual time for a customer to wait in the late 60s for delivery of his order of Rickenbacker guitars. Dick Burke estimates the busiest period as 1965 to 1968, and he recalls a peak of 103 workers at the Rickenbacker factory at the time. The name of the sales and distribution company was changed in 1965 from the old Radio & Television Equipment Co to the more appropriate Rickenbacker Inc, and the sales office was moved in 1966 from South Main to East Stevens in Santa Ana. The name of the manufacturing company remained as Electro String.

More US guitar-makers were drawn to the idea of an electric 12-string. Semie Moseley's Mosrite brand, based in Bakersfield, California, began producing its Ventures solidbody six-string in 1963. A 12-string version with the same distinctively offset body shape appeared two years later. Another California company, the mail-order specialist Carvin, first made electric 12s in 1967, in single or double-neck format.

Gibson launched its ES-335-12 and the Epiphone Riviera 12-string in 1965. Gretsch had made a prototype electric 12 in 1964 intended as a George Harrison model but did not pursue the idea after Harrison showed little enthusiasm. Gretsch's different production model – called, ingeniously, the 12-String – was a double-cutaway hollowbody that appeared in 1966. Guild's acoustic 12-strings were popular, but the company's electric was the Starfire XII of 1966, the same year that Harmony offered its H-79 hollowbody.

More sightings bolstered the case for the strategic use of electric 12-string guitar, with 1966 evidently a key year. You may care to cock an ear to Sean Byrne playing a Danelectro Bellzouki for the relentless rhythm part on Count Five's 'Psychotic Reaction' (a Number 5 single); Jerry McGeorge on jangled Rick rhythm through The Shadows Of Knight's take on 'Gloria' (Number 10); Al Nichol with some more Rick 12 for The Turtles, notably the Top 20 hit 'You Baby'; or Johnny Echols's often-out-of-tune yet entirely appropriate electric 12 on the first Love album.

Later in the 60s, Chris Britton of The Troggs used his later Baldwin version of the Burns Double Six on both sides of the group's 1967 single 'Love Is All Around' and 'When Will The Rain Come': somewhat out-of-tune for the A-side rhythm strumming; more successfully for the flip's riffs. Eric Clapton played an effective Fender Electric XII on Cream's 'Dance The Night Away' on *Disraeli Gears*, while The Velvet Underground deployed a couple of the same guitars in an attempt to enjangle their dirge.

Over at Rickenbacker, one of the consequences of success was that the company

● Other makers joined in with electric 12-string models during the 60s in the wake of Rickenbacker's success. The **Gibson ES-335-12** (main guitar) appeared in 1965, a 12-string version of the revered ES-335.

● **Guild** added the **Starfire XII** in 1966 (below left, centre guitar) while **Harmony** launched its **H-79** the same year (red guitar, right). **Tony Hicks** of The Hollies (below) played a **Vox Phantom XII**.

● For every Beatles and Byrds using electric 12-string guitars in the 60s there were dozens of other groups lining up to add the jangle to their sound. The best known player of the 1966 **Gretsch 12-String** (above) was Michael Nesmith of The Monkees, but **Sean Byrne** of Count V (top, far left) used a Danelectro Bellzouki on the band's insistent hit 'Psychotic Reaction', while **Al Nichol** (right; centre of rear riser) played a Rick 12 on several Turtles cuts.

seemed more willing to indulge inventors with new ideas for guitars. Through the second half of the 60s and into the early 70s, Rickenbacker made a series of bizarre variations on its instruments that most other manufacturers probably wouldn't have allowed to go beyond the drawing-board.

The 'Sceusa neck' was a special asymmetrical neck profile made available on a few guitars. It echoed earlier attempts by makers such as Epiphone, Gretsch, and Burns to provide a shape better suited to the natural arch of the player's hand by exaggerating the curve of the back of the neck toward the bass side. But it felt strange, and like the others the Sceusa neck was not popular. It was soon dropped from Rickenbacker's options. The company's one-year agreement with Peter Sceusa expired in April 1964.

Rickenbacker's string-converter guitars first appeared in 1966. Inventor James E. Gross came up with a converter 'comb' mounted to the body of a 12-string that could be manipulated to remove from play all or some of the second strings of each pair. Gross wrote in his explanatory letter to Rickenbacker of the converter's ability to allow single strings to be used for bass notes while retaining unison pairs for the higher strings "for a dirty 'twang' or mandolin-ish sound".

Gross also said that the converter made the 12-string easier to tune "by starting with the six and then tuning the secondary six to the first six", and that it could facilitate a quick change from 12-string to 6-string (and back) at the flip of a switch. "It would add little cost to production," Gross concluded, "yet would attract a great deal of plus business to the company and the 12-string guitar."

Rickenbacker went ahead with the converter – "Now two guitars in one!" said the publicity – and the July 1966 pricelist showed three models with the chrome converter 'comb' fitted to the body: the 336/12 (in other words a convertible 330/12) at $529.50; the 366/12 (convertible 360/12) at $579.50; and the 456/12 (convertible 450/12) at $339.50. In each case these were priced between $45 and $55 more than the regular versions. There's no evidence that anyone ever found a practical use for the feature in real life.

Another oddity was Quilla H. ('Porky') Freeman's design for a guitar body with invisible pickups, actually situated under the pickguard. Freeman had previously teamed up with Fender, who built prototypes and even featured proposed Marauder guitars in its 1965–66 catalogue, but they never went into production.

Rickenbacker made an agreement with Freeman in 1967, but again the idea did not reach the marketplace. Nonetheless, the company made at least one prototype, an unusual guitar built in April 1968 that did not use any of Rickenbacker's normal body shapes. It had two 'slash' soundholes in a single-cutaway bound body finished in fireglo and a large semi-transparent pickguard under which the four buried pickups could just about be seen.

Slant-fret Rickenbackers first appeared in trial runs at the factory around 1968. Others had tried this, including Stratosphere, and Gretsch, who slanted the frets by one degree above the 12th fret on a couple of models around 1964. Henry C. Perez brought the idea to Rickenbacker, and an agreement was officially completed in 1971. Perez's original sketch dictates an eight-degree slant to frets, pickups, nut, and bridge, with the intention of making the guitar more comfortable to play. Rickenbacker's publicity said: "This slight slant of the frets across the fingerboard eliminates long chord reaches, reduces stretch length, and matches precisely the natural angle of the fretting fingers."

The 1971 pricelist was the first to show the slant-fret option, available on "most models" for an extra $100. Although rarely ordered after the early 70s, it was still noted on pricelists up to 1983. The slant-fret feature was offered as standard on the 481 solidbody, introduced in 1974. Standard colours now were fireglo (red), azureglo (blue), jetglo (black), and burgundyglo (wine red).

F.C. Hall's son John started to work full-time for Rickenbacker in 1969, and he recalls the reaction to the slant-fret guitars. "You pick up a guitar with slanted frets and play it, and it feels great, no question about it. But as soon as you tell someone it's a slanted fret guitar, they look at it, do a double take, oh wow, it is – and then they can't play it any more," he laughs. "We'd sometimes ship slant-fret 360s to people who ordered a 360, and then we'd never hear anything from them. I think our general feeling was, well, if no one cares, forget it."

Last of the decidedly weird Rickenbackers were the lightshow guitars, introduced as the 331 and 331/12 models in 1970. They each had a clear plastic top through which a psychedelic array of coloured lights would shine, flashing in response to the frequencies of the notes that the guitarist played. They came with a special unit that plugged between guitar and amplifier.

"This was a three-channel colour organ," explains John Hall. "The three light circuits were sensitive in different frequency ranges: if low frequency notes were hit, the lowest channel would trigger and whatever colour lights were screwed into that channel would blink. Mid and high frequencies lit the other channels. The whole combination of them, in a chord for instance, would mean they didn't light."[57]

The lightshow system was introduced to the company by Stephen F. Woodman and Marshall Arm, although Rickenbacker modified the original design by developing its own printed circuit boards and adding silver-foil lining inside the body to increase the projection of the bulbs. The instrument proved unpredictable, especially as a result of over-heating, and the experience of using one has since been likened to playing a toaster with pickups.

Roger McGuinn had a special 12-string lightshow guitar built with slant frets and three pickups, which he would use for 'Eight Miles High' at the end of Byrds shows in the early 70s. It was perhaps the most bizarre Rickenbacker ever made – a rare prize indeed, given the number of oddities made at the factory in Santa Ana.

In 1966, Rickenbacker introduced a revised series of six-string Thin Full-Body models, the originals of which had been dropped a few years earlier. Only the deluxe models – 360F, 365F, 370F, and 375F – were redesigned and, a little later, a 12-string 360/12F was

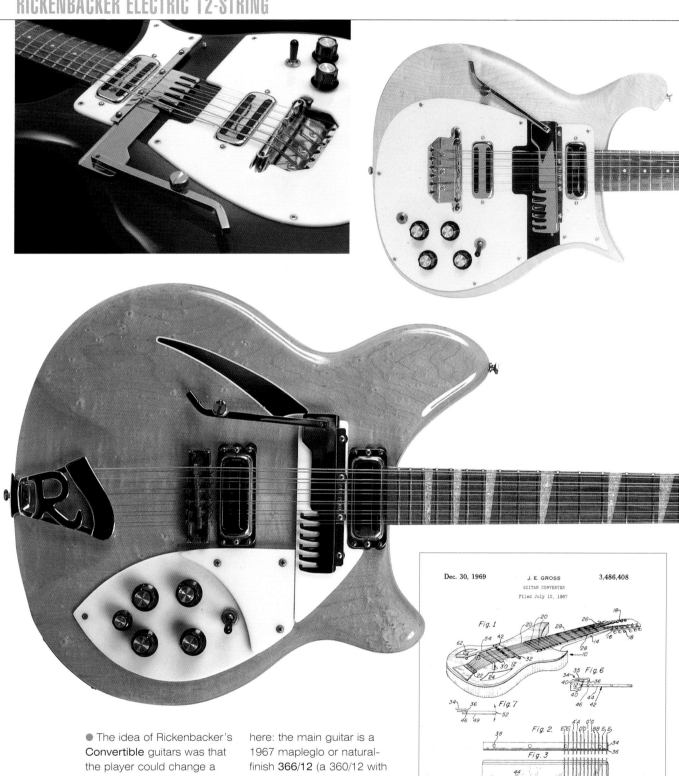

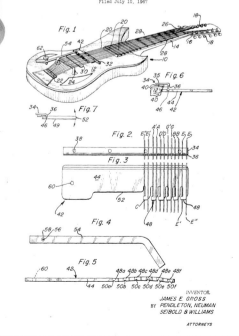

● The idea of Rickenbacker's **Convertible** guitars was that the player could change a 12-string to a 6-string and back again at the flick of a 'converter' switch. The inventor was one James Gross, whose **patent** for the design is shown (right). A few examples of the models put into production are pictured here: the main guitar is a 1967 mapleglo or natural-finish **366/12** (a 360/12 with converter) and at the top of the page is a 1968 **456/12** (a 450/12 with converter). The close-up (top left) details another 456/12 and the "comb" and "teeth" of its converter system. These odd guitars were not a success.

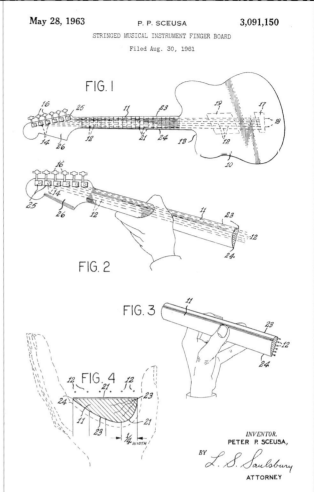

May 28, 1963   P. P. SCEUSA   3,091,150
STRINGED MUSICAL INSTRUMENT FINGER BOARD
Filed Aug. 30, 1961

FIG. I

FIG. 2

FIG. 3

FIG. 4

INVENTOR.
PETER P. SCEUSA,
BY
L. S. Saulsbury
ATTORNEY

● Peter Sceusa's early-60s idea for an asymmetrical neck profile (**patent**, right) did not live up to the hype, and Rickenbacker's deal with him was shortlived. The lightshow guitars, the 331 (1971 example, bottom of page) and the 331/12, were spectacular: lamps with coloured filters in the body, flashing to a changing pattern, were visible through the transparent top. Made in the early 70s, the lightshow guitars, too, did not last. Five 12s at a **1967 trade show** (below right) offered a "new dimension in sound" (left to right): 450/12; 330/12; 360/12 new-style; 360/12 old-style; and 360/12F.

added. The new F models had controls laid out in a curving line near the edge of the body, no longer mounted on a pickguard. Dick Burke remembers that F.C. Hall asked for such an arrangement and that once again it fell to Burke to find a solution.

He had to come up with a way of getting the controls mounted on the body without gaining access to the semi-hollow body from the back. "So we made a special hole about two-and-a-half inches in diameter under the big pickguard," Burke recalls. "We would feed the controls into that hole and then, just like a surgeon, use a long tool to pull each one through the small individual holes on the body, locking them into position."[58] The new style of F models was released during 1966.

Meanwhile, one American band that took to the electric 12-string with enthusiasm was Jefferson Airplane, whose rhythm guitarist Paul Kantner played a Rickenbacker 360/12. "I'm really fond of the 12-string in general, ever since I came upon it in my early days," he says today. "It makes me sound like an entire orchestra, to my ear."

Kantner came to the Airplane with a Guild acoustic 12-string fitted with a pickup but soon acquired his first Rick 12. Not that he stopped playing acoustic 12 – "just strumming a chord on a 12-string is an amazing thing" – but an electric was essential for high-powered work with his band. "I must say, because my hands are fairly thick German worker's hands rather than elegant piano-player kind of hands, it took me many years to get them used to that very small neck the Rickenbacker has. But compared to acoustic 12s, Rickenbackers are relatively easy to play in terms of pressure and tension."

The Rick 12 became an important part of the sound of Jefferson Airplane. "I was fond of not having my 12-string rhythm guitar way out front like a lot of 12-string electric players do, particularly lead players. I was more content with creating a nice thick sound in combination with the bass and, when we had it, the piano player, starting with Grace Slick and then Nicky Hopkins and others. I liked the lower end of the 12-string: that's the place I like to be. Down at the low notes and the lower parts of the chords is where I get my best sound. I would strive to make a combination of elements rather than a solo kind of situation."

He's aware that some see 'rhythm guitarist' as a limiting term but explains that he's not like most members of the genre anyway. "Usually they play in a blues mode. I'm a white boy, and I have no interest whatsoever in the blues. I was raised on folk, things like The Weavers, Pete Seeger's band – that reverence for songs with harmonies, songs that came out of the American folk tradition. Jefferson Airplane was a combination: we had two great blues players, Jack Casady and Jorma Kaukonen, and we had myself and Marty Balin as the folkies. We had two extraordinary vocalists, too, and I sort of stuck my vocals in there and made a three-part out of it. It made for a unique sound overall."

Kantner points to the band's *Volunteers* album of 1969 as a highlight for his playing, from the opening chords of the title track onward. "A lot of times on recordings I would combine Rickenbacker with an acoustic 12-string and use both of them to give a broader sweep. I still do that today – I'll combine the two when we record. I haven't found the way to play two 12-strings on stage yet, but if I could I would." He's keen on open tunings for his 12s – which brings to mind the first Jefferson Starship album, *Blows Against The Empire,* released in 1970. "Quite a few songs on that album are in I think open D, and within that structure, as you go up the neck, you can play all kinds of random variations of chords, leaving the open strings ringing both on the high and the low end. You can build chords in amongst that which really sound beautiful."[59]

At Rickenbacker, Dick Burke reckons it was about this time that demand for the company's guitars began to decline. He estimates that the slower years were 1969, 1970, and 1971. From a peak of just over 100 factory workers at one point during the busy 1965–1968 period, there was a time between 1969 and 1971 when just eight workers were employed at the factory, he recalls.

A few changes were made to the guitar models at this time. In 1969, a new type of high-output pickup called the Hi-Gain was introduced. The same year saw the introduction of 24 frets for the family of 300-series guitars, which until then had 21 frets as standard. Production of both 21-fret and 24-fret models continued into the 70s, but by the middle of the decade the 21-fret versions had all but disappeared. A modern-style version of the 381 appeared, and a 12-string version, the 381/12, was added to the line.

Around 1970, the deluxe 'triangle' fingerboard inlay was made less wide, as Dick Burke remembers. "We changed it at that time from all the way across to mid-way. I think it makes for a stronger neck when the inlay doesn't go all the way across, especially on a 12-string. On the older version, we used to take more wood out, and that would weaken the neck." In the mid 70s, Rickenbacker stopped equipping guitars with the Ac'cent vibrato and did not reinstate this unit until 1985.

In the early 70s, Rickenbacker introduced what for the company was a radically different design, its first new body shape for many years, and which unusually for Rickenbacker was teamed with a bolt-on neck. The solidbody design finally appeared in public as the model 430, launched in 1971 as a lower-cost guitar ($249.50), a reaction to cheaper imported guitars.

The 430 was based on tooling developed for a proposed line of models devised by Forrest White, who worked briefly for Rickenbacker around 1970. White had been production chief at Fender from 1954 to 1967, and so it's not surprising that the styling of the 430 is closer to Fender than anything Rickenbacker had made previously. It did not prove a success: it was neither classic Rickenbacker nor especially exciting.

Another new body shape appeared at this time, although it was really only new to Rickenbacker's six-string guitar lines. The 480 six-string, introduced in 1973, used the body styling made famous by the company's basses, which had first appeared in 1957. The most distinctive visual aspect was an elongated left horn, and the idea to produce a guitar version was probably F.C. Hall's. Dick Burke says that, given the great popularity of Rickenbacker's basses in the early 70s, marketing sense dictated a guitar version. "It would look good if the guys were playing both in a band," he says. "I guess Mr Hall felt that if

With *Rickenbacker* **steppenwolf** can tell it like it really is

Steppenwolf music is a wild, wild 'hard rock' wind blowing throughout the land. And, the "heavy" sound of Steppenwolf all starts with Rickenbacker guitars and amps. You'd better believe John Kay, Mike Monarch, and Nick St. Nicholas keep close watch on those Rickenbackers between sets.

Steppenwolf's on tour right now. Check in at your local Rickenbacker dealer's showroom — see if Steppenwolf will be visiting your area. While you're there, have him show you the finest guitars and amps that money can buy. The kind the pro's depend on . . .

Rickenbacker

World's Most Distinguished Name In Guitars, Amplifiers and Accessories
P.O. Box 2275 • 201 East Stevens Street
Dept. "Q" • Santa Ana, Calif. 92707 • (714) 545-5574

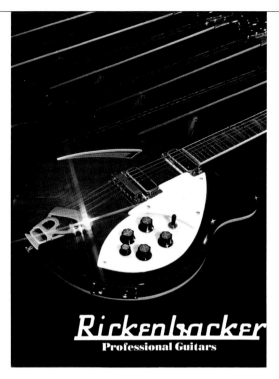

Rickenbacker
Professional Guitars

● Steppenwolf joined a promo tour for Rickenbacker in 1968 (tour bus, top left, and flyer, left). The 1975 catalogue (above) shows new Hi-Gain pickups, a 24-fret neck, and less-wide fingerboard markers.

● Paul Kantner of Jefferson Airplane (above) enjoyed using his Rickenbacker 360/12 for the rhythm-guitar work he contributed to the band. The picture shows him at the fated Altamont festival in 1969, complete with psychedelic decoration to his amp and cabinets – but relatively restrained personalisation to his guitar. That same year saw the introduction of a new Rickenbacker 12-string model, the **381/12**. The example shown (above left) is one of Rickenbacker's V69 reissues of the model, this one dating from 1993.

● Rickenbacker's "F" deluxe models were revised in 1966 with a shallower cutaway and a new control layout, as on this 1968 **360/12F** (main guitar). Rick usually mounted controls on the pickguard, but for these new Thin Full-Body models the knobs were relocated to the body rim for a stylish look. Some examples of the 12-string appeared before its official launch in 1973.

87

you had a guitar that was similar it might sell the instrument along with the bass."[60] A year later the 481 was added, with slanted frets and a pair of humbucking pickups. It provided another less-than-popular outing for Henry Perez's new angle on fretting. In 1980, the three-pickup 483 was added to the bass-body family. They stayed in the line until 1983, which saw a 12-string version of the 340 (effectively a three-pickup 330/12).

The company's valuable link with The Beatles was naturally severed when that group split in 1970. Little in the way of new Rickenbacker models was forthcoming to excite guitar players, and the fashionable instrument of the time was the Gibson Les Paul. Fortunately for Rickenbacker, its bass guitars gained in popularity in the early 70s after bassists such as Chris Squire of Yes were seen using them, and production began to pick up again at Santa Ana, concentrating on four-string models.

In the US in the early 70s, Tim Buckley was seen on stage with a Fender Electric XII, replacing his more familiar Guild acoustic 12, while the pop tradition of jangling Rickenbacker 12 was upheld by Wally Bryson of The Raspberries on their hits 'I Wanna Be With You' and 'Let's Pretend'. John McLaughlin used Gibson and Rex Bogue double-necks with 12-string during the life of his jazz-rock band The Mahavishnu Orchestra.

In Britain, Jimmy Page used probably a Fender Electric XII to record the rhythm part on Led Zeppelin's 'Stairway To Heaven' early in 1971. He brings in his electric 12 just under half way through to strengthen the fingerpicked acoustic that opens the track. Page soon acquired a Gibson EDS-1275 6-and-12 double-neck to play the song live. Charlie Whitney of Family used an EDS 1275 throughout the band's career – boosted when a record deal led to their first album, *Music In A Doll's House*, in 1968 – until their split in 1973. Several British prog-rock bands of the 70s used electric 12s, including Caravan (Pye Hastings with a Fender Electric XII), Genesis (Mike Rutherford with bass-and-12 double-necks by Rickenbacker or Shergold), and Yes (Steve Howe with EDS-1275 double-neck or Rickenbacker 360/12).

Another British band, Starry Eyed And Laughing, made a mark with the very Byrds-like sound of a Rick 12-string. They started in London pubs, were signed to CBS in 1974, and recorded their debut self-titled album with American producer Dan Loggins. There was no doubt about the primary influence on Starry Eyed And Laughing, recalls guitarist Tony Poole. "Our original inspiration was the original five Byrds. With 'Mr Tambourine Man' and their first album, you were just drawn in by that drone-like sound."

Poole started the band playing an old acoustic 12. Acquiring management meant money for gear, and he knew exactly what he wanted. "I got my guitar down in Tin Pan Alley – Denmark Street, in central London – probably in early '74. It was a 1967 Rickenbacker 330/12 and cost £240, which I paid in instalments. It was the one with the square-ish body, which I'd always coveted – the rounded one didn't seem so nice. It was black, which was kind of cool for a pub-rock band, and according to the shop the one previous owner was Steve Peregrine-Took, *not* the guitarist from Tyrannosaurus Rex. God knows what he was doing with it."

Familiar with a 12-string acoustic, Poole assumed that someone had strung his 330/12 the wrong way around and changed it to a thin-string-on-top layout. Later he realised he'd changed Rickenbacker's unconventional method, but liked it too much to change back.

He was disappointed with one aspect of his new guitar, which suffered from low output. "I'd crank it up and put as much treble on as I could, but never got that Byrds sound, not initially," Poole recalls. "I'd seen it played by Roger McGuinn and thought it was going to be instant Byrds – but in fact my little old Suzuki acoustic 12 was probably more jangly." A schoolfriend who knew about electronics suggested bypassing the passive tone control and feeding direct from the pickups. "That was a breakthrough for me," grins Poole. "Suddenly it had level that could drive an amp."

He says the first time he got the compressed Rick 12 sound was the first time they went into the CBS studios in London. The engineer on the first Starry Eyed sessions was Mike Ross, who'd recorded the Clarence White edition of The Byrds the year before at CBS London for the *Farther Along* album. Columbia had flown over some copy-masters of the first Byrds album as a reference for Ross. "So we're in the studio there recording our first session ever," recalls Poole, "and the guy gets the master box from the basement archive. It was amazing hearing that coming out of those speakers."

The Rick 12 can dominate a mix. "That's probably the 12-string's strength," says Poole. "If you're going to record it, you have to build the track around it. I think of the R.E.M. tracks that work like that. There's an awful lot of bands that use them, but I often find that if the Rick is not centre-stage, then it wastes the sound. You diminish that jangle."

Poole did not diminish the jangle with Starry Eyed And Laughing. Playing with a plectrum and two fingerpicks, he often put his Rick 330/12 centre-stage. On the first album, 'Lady Came From The South' has him soloing through a phase shifter. His 12 is prominent on the intro of 'See Your Face' and dances around the solo of 'Nobody Home'. On the second LP, less Byrdsian, there's still room for some classic Rick 12 on tracks like 'One Foot In The Boat' and 'Down The Street'.

The paired strings of an electric 12-string don't always imply modern settings to the guitarist or the listener. "The instrument also has that slightly medieval quality about it, going back to lutes and so on," says Poole. "There's something that speaks to people who don't know anything about guitars, something about that mystical combination of harmonics and overtones. There's this spiritual thing that results. I think The Byrds hooked into that with recordings like 'Why'. Maybe that medieval quality just speaks to something inside us."[61]

Back at Rickenbacker, the company had made a few custom double-neck guitars for individual guitarists in the 60s, but in 1975 its first production double-necks appeared. There were two types: the 4080 bass-and-12 and 4080/12 6-and-12 were modelled on the company's classic bass-body style; the 362/12 enlarged upon the familiar 360 design.

Double-neck electric guitars had been made since the early 50s by various companies – earlier, we met one of the first, the Stratosphere. The main aim was to provide two guitars

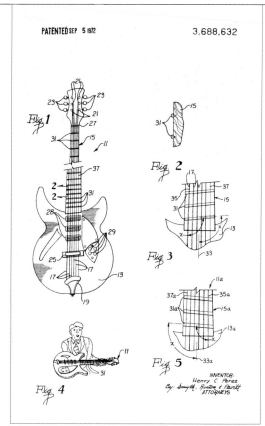

PATENTED SEP 5 1972   3,688,632

● For a while the Fender Electric XII looked like the main competition for Rickenbacker's 12-strings. Of course, the Fender was a solidbody: that and its familiar playability attracted a number of players, including **Tim Buckley** (top left), who used its electric qualities as an alternative to his acoustic Guild 12-string.

● This slant-fret 1976 **481** (main guitar) and the regular 480 had a body based on Rick's popular bass guitars. **Slanted frets** were brought to Rickenbacker by Henry Perez (**patent**, top). The slanting was supposed to improve playability, but the idea did not last. Fortunately, Rick did not attempt a slant-fret 12-string.

● **Double-neck** electrics have been around at least since the 50s Stratosphere. Rickenbacker introduced its own models in 1975 (see page 94), inspired by **Mike Rutherford** of Genesis (above) who had Roger Giffin make a custom job that combined a Rick bass and 12-string. More double-neck fans here: **John McLaughlin** with his Mahavishnu Orchestra (top right) and a Rex Bogue 12 and 6, and **Jimmy Page** in Led Zeppelin (right) with his Gibson EDS-1275, also pairing 12 and 6-string.

in one, usually a combination of 6-string guitar and 4-string bass, or 6-string and 12-string guitars. Of course, the resulting instruments were heavy, and most players would necessarily limit their stage use of double-necks to a few appropriate songs.

Roger McGuinn had one of the earliest 362 double-necks, built for him before the official production run started, and he echoes the general feeling about such instruments. "I got mine in 1972. I found it a little too heavy to use for the whole show and would use my 370/12 for the most part."[62] Rickenbacker's double-necks were expensive and manufactured in very small batches: Dick Burke recalls that they would make as few as 10 or 15 at a time.

In March 1976, Adolph Rickenbacker died at the age of 89. He had not been involved with the guitar company for over 20 years. Two years later, Rickenbacker Inc moved offices, again within Santa Ana, from East Stevens to South Main, while the factory stayed at the same location on Kilson where it had been situated since the move from Los Angeles that had happened in 1962.

The January 1978 pricelist listed 21 electric guitar models under three headings. *Electric Solid Body*: 420 $299; 430 $325; 450 $390; 450/12 $475; 460 $490; 480 $415; 481 $575; 620 $548; 900 $305; 950 $400; 4080 $1350; 4080/12 $1750.

Electric Thin Hollow Body: 320 $565; 330 $550; 330/12 $725; 340 $570; 360 $650; 360/12 $770; 362/12 $1500; 370 $690.

Electric Thin Full Body: 360/12F $638.

Meanwhile, following another peak in the mid 70s, demand for Rickenbacker's instruments had again declined. Dick Burke recalls that by the early 80s, the workforce at Kilson was down to some 20 or 30 people.

The market in so-called vintage guitars had been building since the late 60s. Some instruments were achieving high prices, especially as a result of successful (and wealthy) guitarists choosing to redistribute some of their earnings among eager vintage guitar dealers. Rickenbackers were by no means top of the list of vintage desirables, but nonetheless examples of the company's output from the 50s and 60s were beginning to fetch increasing sums.

In 1983, Rickenbacker made a half-hearted attempt to recreate some of its older models, trying to capture some of the vintage market, and produced the disappointingly inaccurate B-series models: the 360/12B ($1140), 320B ($1085), and 325B ($1185), as well as a bass. Another nod to its past occurred the same year with the 350 Liverpool ($820) and 355 Liverpool Plus ($920), which were full-scale, 24-fret versions of the short-scale 325-style guitar associated with John Lennon – hence the Liverpool tag.

One of the most distinctive outings for a Rickenbacker electric 12 at the time came with XTC's *English Settlement* album, released in 1982. "I can't think of any other English bands then who'd exploited the sound quite as fully as we did with that record," says guitarist Dave Gregory. "And my Rickenbacker was a new toy for me."

Gregory bought a black 1976 360/12 from singer-songwriter Andy Desmond in 1981.

It cost him £300 (plus £20 for a parking ticket). When he got it home and plugged it in, he heard an extraordinary sound. "I thought: why have I waited so long to get one of these? I couldn't stop playing it," Gregory recalls, "and I took it down to rehearsals for *Settlement*. It inspired the others to go back and listen to 60s pop like The Byrds and The Beatles, which they'd only really dipped their toes into. I think Andy Partridge was more familiar with The Beatles, but he didn't know anything about The Byrds. They went for it straight away. Colin Moulding got a fretless bass, so we had acoustic guitar, 12-string Rick, and fretless bass – about as far away from our previous album, *Black Sea*, as you could be."

Gregory loved that his Rick 12 was not an obvious lead guitar and didn't have a big rock sound. "It made a nice foil for Terry Chambers's heavy drums and Andy's spikey electric guitar, and a 12-string and an acoustic together made for a great texture." The album was all about texture. "I think it signalled the direction of the band for the next couple of albums. It was an arresting new sound for us: not rock'n'roll, and miles away from the FM synthesizers and disco that everyone else seemed to be doing. And it stamped my personality firmly on the record."

That 12-string stamp is clearly evident on 'Senses Working Overtime', 'Jason And The Argonauts', and 'All Of A Sudden', full of those ringing, chiming, jangling arpeggios. "I've become a bit of a walking arpeggiating cliché in my time," admits Gregory, "but I don't mind that, because I love an arpeggio. When you leave the top two strings on a Rick 12 and move down, you have that octave thing coming in with the other strings – and that puts a whole new spin on an arpeggio. You're just not quite sure what's going on."

Watch your Gs, says Gregory. "You have to tune the lower G of the pair about a quarter-tone flat, because when you start fretting with the octave string, for some reason they nearly always blow sharp. I try to avoid open Gs, so that when they're fretted they're closer in tune. I've noticed this with other 12-string players: they nearly always ask their guitar techs to tune the lower string of the Gs just a tiny bit flat."

XTC changed as drummer Chambers left and Partridge couldn't tour. *Mummer* in 1983 had some 12-string moments – 'Deliver Us From The Elements' and 'Funk Pop A Roll' – but 'Beating Of Hearts' was something special. Partridge decided to tune all the strings on his guitar to E and play an eastern motif. "I tuned all 12 strings of my Rickenbacker to E," reports Gregory. "It sounded fantastic. I thought it had to be the next single: it just sounded so odd but so great, this ridiculous tuning with no regard for traditional guitar-playing methods. The guitar had become just a thing to make a sound. It was a joy."

Gregory retired his 360/12 in 1983 because he managed to get close to his ideal 12 in the shape of a Rick Rose-Morris 1993 model. First, though, he'd written a cheeky letter to George Harrison. "I asked if he still had the *Hard Day's Night* Rickenbacker and would he consider selling it? It came back with his handwritten notes – 'George' crossed out and 'Dave' written in. It was like an email where you get indents: he just put a pen through it and wrote underneath.

"I said I'd been looking for so long for one that looks like yours, and I don't like the

● This black 1976 **360/12** is owned by **Dave Gregory**, who used it on XTC's 1982 album *English Settlement* and a number of subsequent records as well. He replaced it in the early 80s with a Rose-Morris model 1993.

● Rickenbacker moved its **factory** in the late 80s to the current spot at the corner of South Main and Stevens in Santa Ana, California. This photo (right) was taken soon after the relocation.

● **Double-necks** first appeared on the Rick pricelist in 1975. Shown here are a 1979 **362/12** (bottom left), in 360 style and combining 12-string and 6-string necks, and a 1981 **4080/12** (centre), which pairs bass and 12-string necks. The 1974 **330** (this page) was owned and played by **Paul Weller** of The Jam, a keen Rick fan who scratched the punk-ish message into its top. In the 80s, Rickenbacker began to produce a **Vintage** oldies series, summed up in the moody shot on this 1984 **catalogue** cover (above).

way the new ones look too much. 'I know what you mean,' he wrote under that. So, I asked, would there be any chance, if you still have it, that you might be prepared to sell it to me? I'm about to do a new album with my band, XTC. 'No, sorry.' It must have been February of 1981, because I added a PS wishing him a happy birthday. 'Thanks very much.' I had no idea there were only three Rickenbackers like that. There was the one for the country and western singer, with the cooker knobs, George's was the second, and then they made one for Gerry Marsden."

So, with a Beatle-shape no for his trouble, Gregory put another ad in *Melody Maker*, made another trip to London, and finally ended up with his Rose-Morris 1993. He didn't know then that these are rare guitars, too, and so he began to get picky with the seller, who hadn't mentioned the headstock break. "I said look, no pickguard, noisy pots – and he was getting a bit sheepish by now. So I tipped it over to look at the serial number: it's DG 952. DG? That's me. My date of birth? September 1952. £300? Done."

A head repair, a clean-up, and Gregory had himself a new arpeggio machine. He pressed the Rose-Morris 1993 into service on every record that XTC made after that. Savour some more 12-string moments on 'Train Running Low On Slow Coal' on *Big Express*, 'You're My Drug' on *Psonic Psunspot* by The Dukes Of Stratosphear (a pseudonym for the group's psychedelic research), 'Earn Enough For Us' on *Skylarking*, and 'Mayor Of Simpleton' on *Oranges & Lemons*.

"A little of the Rick 12 sound goes a long way," says Gregory. "It puts you in a place as soon as you hear just a couple of notes on it, and you stay there until the record's over. It inspires a kind of subconscious relocation of the listener's senses."[63]

Meanwhile in the 80s, Rickenbacker revived the body shape it had used for the 430, launching in 1983 the 230 Hamburg and 250 El Dorado models. Suddenly Rickenbacker guitars had model names! "That was something I really wanted to do. After all, every other company had names," laughs John Hall. "These instruments were feeling like bastards, with no names of their own. So we started thinking, and since then we've given names to the new instruments – as well as numbers, of course."

As with the 430, the idea for the Hamburg and El Dorado was to make a lower-cost simple-looking guitar, and again Rickenbacker used the cheaper bolt-on-neck method of construction. Hall collaborated with Rickenbacker's electronic engineer, George Cole, to come up with a clever electronic tweak. "They have passive boost circuits," Hall explains. "We sacrificed some of the power coming off the high-output pickups to drive the boost, instead of using a battery. The trouble was that the treble pickup didn't have all of that extra power. You could light up a flashlight bulb with the bass pickup, there was so much power. But the treble pickup was never quite as effective."

Another band whose work makes good use of 12-string is The Church. The Anglo-Australian outfit's biggest hit would come with 'Under The Milky Way' in 1988, but from their first album, 1981's *Of Skins And Heart*, to their latest, 2009's *Untitled #23*, guitarist Marty Willson-Piper has always looked for new settings and fresh voices for his electric

12s. "A lot of people use the Ricky 12-string in an arpeggio sense, and that's what it's famous for," he says. "But that's just not how I use it."

The electric 12 should not be an instrument you pull out for the odd song, according to Willson-Piper. "A lot of people use it like that. But it's something else. I don't say oh, now it's time for the novelty song! Let's get the 12 – let's do the jangly one. I do songs that I have to play intricate or interesting or melodic arpeggio parts. It's not necessarily a 12-string part – I play that part on the six-string. The 12 is for songs where I need the 12. Not just for jangly arpeggios."

His favourite for some time has been a Rickenbacker 370/12RM Roger McGuinn model. "I use it as a rock guitar. I throw that thing around and play power chords on it and do screaming solos on it. 'Tantalized', for example, is a crazy, indelicate song. You'd think I'd be using a Les Paul or something, but it's Rick 12. For the solo at the end, live, I use the 12 for a ripping solo with a wah-wah and a fuzz box."

Not your average Rick sound – and more examples of Willson-Piper's broader intentions for electric 12 include the glorious sheets of sound on 'Columbus' from *Heyday* (1985) and 'North South East And West' from *Starfish* (1988). "On that, Peter [Koppes] plays the intro rhythm part, and then I come in with a fuzz box playing this scale run, not an arpeggio at all. The solo is double-speed fast stuff with a fuzz box. So yes, I think the Rickenbacker 12 is such an underused instrument."

His first electric guitar was a Rickenbacker six-string, but when he joined The Church in 1980 he got a mapleglo '65 330/12. Willson-Piper – who was born in Liverpool, lived in London for a while, and moved to Australia for The Church – switched the string pairs around on his 330 to non-Rick style, with the heavy string 'underneath' the octave string. He's had other 12s – a Burns Double Six that can be heard on songs like 'Is This Where You Live' on *Skins And Hearts*, and a Shergold double-neck – but mostly his heart is Rickenbacker shaped.

"When you play a Rick 12-string," he explains, "it isn't workmanlike: it's got finesse, it's subtler, it's more aesthetically pleasing, it's got quality about it. It's like getting out of a Ford and into a nicer car. The Gibsons and things are like the BMWs and the Mercs, where the Rick is more like an Aston Martin. A higher level."[64]

Rickenbacker's business operation changed fundamentally when John Hall officially took control in 1984, by which time F.C. Hall was 76 and ready to hand over the reins to his son. John formed a new company, Rickenbacker International Corporation (RIC), which purchased the guitar-related parts of his father's Rickenbacker Inc and Electro String companies. Rickenbacker Inc also had oil and land holdings, and Electro had other property. By 2009, John had done some technical manoeuvring so that RIC is in fact the original Electro String company – "a nod to the history" as he puts it.[65]

With the new set-up in place, Hall started to change the sales organisation of the company. He established offices in England and Japan and instituted a proper vintage reissue programme. The first results of this appeared in 1984 with the 325V59, 325V63,

● These candid backstage shots (left) show a couple of the Ricks belonging to R.E.M. guitarist **Peter Buck**. Far left is a **660/12**, his recent stage 12-string, and next to that is Buck's beloved **360**, which he's used on almost every record the band has ever made. Pictured opposite: a 1992 **250 El Dorado**, an attempt to make a more modern Rick, discontinued that year; Church guitarist **Marty Willson-Piper** with his 370/12 McGuinn model; and a descriptive **colour key** from the 1982 catalogue.

● Rickenbacker's Vintage series got into proper gear in 1984 and has been successful ever since. One of the first instruments in the reissue programme was this **360/12V64** (main guitar), which aimed to reproduce the charm, playability, and unusual details of the first 12-string that George Harrison played in the 60s. (It has since been renamed the 360/12C63.) Two Rickenbacker kings are pictured on stage together (left): **Peter Buck** with his 360 and **Johnny Marr** with his 370/12 McGuinn.

COLOR KEY

STANDARD

FG (Fire-glo)	BG (Burgundy)	JG (Jet-glo)	AG (Azure-glo)

CUSTOM (Glossy Finish)

RBY (Ruby)	WAL (Walnut)	MG (Maple-glo)	WHT (White)

CUSTOM (Matte Finish)

NAT (Natural)	BLK (Black)	BRN (Brown)

OPTIONS: WB - Binding Both Sides   LH - Left-handed   WT - White Trim
FL - Fretless   CB - Check Binding   BT - Black Trim

Models 3000, 3001 and 430 - only matte black and matte brown are standard colors.
All other colors on these models have custom-charge.

**** INSTRUMENT COLOR MAY VARY DUE TO THE HAND FINISHING PROCESS ****

and 360/12V64 models. "It was my goal to recreate very accurately those early guitars," says Hall. "I also came up with that numbering system, to allow for the fact that many of these guitars were the same model but were very different from year to year.

"For the 325, we had to do a V59 and a V63 – a Vintage 1959 and a Vintage 1963. Even though it was really the same guitar, a process of evolution had worked upon the instruments a little bit. So the number system was created to reflect that, and to allow us some flexibility to be able to reissue the same model of guitar but from different eras."

Since the first reissues, Hall has altered some of these date-names as new information has come to light. Those vintage 325 models, for example, were rendered more recently as a V58 and a V64.

Hall did a good deal of research, looking at old photos, company records, and original instruments, some of which Rickenbacker had in its own collection – a rarity among modern guitar companies. "Fortunately, in many cases we had the existing tooling, too," he says, "although in a lot of cases it was not marked. So it was a matter of finding an original guitar, holding it up to the patterns we have, and saying ah-ha, that's the one.

"I also sensed that we were more famous for what we had done than what we were doing – and at that particular time I'd say we were stagnant. But when I took over, I had a lot more energy and wanted to take the thing a lot further, a lot faster, so it was fine for me to start tinkering with the formula. In that respect, the vintage reissues made a lot of sense – and there were certainly many people asking us for guitars like that."[66]

Dick Burke helped to redesign the company's truss-rod system. "We changed to two single rods in the necks rather than the two double rods," he explains. "It's a much better system." With small improvements, the new system continues today. A more visible change in 1985 resulted from Rickenbacker's revival of vibrato-equipped models after a break of some ten years. The company manufactured the 'new' Ac'cent-style units in-house. So for example the 615 reappeared briefly, and around the same time Rickenbacker concocted 'new' vibrato-less equivalents, the 610 and 610/12.

Yet another important name in Rickenbacker history is R.E.M., the band from Athens, Georgia, whose music has always been full of Ricks, both twelve and six. Guitarist Peter Buck bought his first Rickenbacker in 1980, a mapleglo six-string, but it was stolen about a year later. It was then that he got his beloved black 360 six-string.

"I was in Hartford, Connecticut, doing a show for $100, and that blond guitar was stolen from the van or someone's apartment or something," Buck recalls. "So we went to a tiny little guitar shop and pulled a new Rick out of a box. It was in tune," he laughs. "Played it, it sounded great – and it's the one I've used on every single record I've ever made, except the 'Radio Free Europe' single, and on every tour to some degree or another – I think there was one in '85 where I didn't use it for a bit. I've played that guitar on stage and in the studio my entire adult life."

His black 360 has an un-lacquered ebony fingerboard, he's added a brass bridge, and he uses what he describes as "super-heavy strings". Specifically, 13 on the high end to 58 on the low. This can pose a problem for anyone other than Buck who tries to play his guitar. Scott McCaughey, who plays with Buck in Robyn Hitchcock & The Venus 3, has been one victim.

"If I'm late for the soundcheck – which I never am – but if I'm doing something or if I'm sick and missing, Scott will go over to test my rig, and he always says: I cannot play your guitar! To him, it sounds horrible," Buck says, smiling. "It takes a huge amount of pressure to push down the strings. I actually bend them up, like, three steps. Honestly, I lend my guitar to people, and they'll say how on earth do you play that? But I'm a rhythm guitar player – and the thicker the string, the better the tone."

For Buck, there was a resonance around Rickenbacker that came from an awareness of the history. "Knowing that Roger McGuinn and George Harrison and Pete Townshend played them – that's kind of the trifecta. Rickenbackers have a very nice distinctive shape – and they haven't changed shape over the years."

Buck likes this continuity about Rickenbacker. "They're the only major guitar company in the world that makes them exactly the same way they did 50 years ago," he says. "They don't have an assembly line. The company hasn't been sold to anyone. That makes the new ones just as good as the old ones. But they're not all the same – they're all a little different. You could play 20 of the exact same model and they're going to sound different. You don't get the identikit sound that you get with some guitars."

When it came time to get a 12-string, Buck reckons he probably used a Fender Electric XII for the first couple of R.E.M. albums, *Murmur* (1983) and *Reckoning* (1984). "I would have loved a Rickenbacker 12 in those days, but they were super-rare as far as getting them used, and I just had no money. I was making like $100 a month, so for me to go out and buy a $1,500 guitar just wasn't going to be. I ended up getting one some time in the mid 80s and I've used them a bunch. I love the McGuinn model, that's a really nice one, and I've got the Tom Petty model."

Buck doesn't like to over-use electric 12. "But if I do use one, it tends to be something that totally lifts the song at the chorus. I've found it's not something I want to use when I'm strumming chords or playing super-single lines, I want it to be arpeggios and broken chords and riffs and stuff. That tends to work, and then I'll usually try it on 12-string if I'm doing overdubs."

Sometimes Buck's 12-string arpeggios almost become a solo, even if not a traditional solo – as with something like 'Texarkana' from 1991's *Out Of Time*. "If I'm not doing a solo but I want to get a melody in there," he explains, "doing an arpeggio means I can really work a lot of melodies in. It doesn't sound as if you're soloing against the vocal. So I tend to use that as a way to add in extra melodic stuff.

"Also, you can get a really great sound by getting a 12 really fuzzy and just playing one string. On 'Time After Time' on our second record I did that. Because of the double strings, it just filled up a lot of space. Double the solo on 12-string and put it underneath – it adds a little kick to it."

● This 1988 **370/12RME1** is a prototype that resides in the Rickenbacker collection. The company is a rarity among modern guitar-makers in that it has changed hands only once in its history, and the collection of significant models that Rickenbacker has built up over the years is the source of a good number of the guitars illustrated in these pages.

● **Roger McGuinn**'s signature model Rickenbacker 12-string was introduced in 1988 as the **370/12RME1**, and the limited edition of 1,000 had sold out by the following year. The first Rickenbacker signature guitar had been 1987's Pete Townshend model (see page 110), but the McGuinn created a great deal of interest among 12-string fans and has since become a desirable player's guitar. The three examples pictured here show the three finishes in which the McGuinn was offered: mapleglo, or natural (below), fireglo, or red sunburst (above), and jetglo, or black (right). McGuinn's first thought when Rick boss John Hall put the idea to him was for the guitar to have an onboard compressor, and Bob Dessidaro designed the circuit that ended up in the instrument. Another key feature is the 12-saddle bridge, which at the time was a first for a Rick 12. Roger McGuinn is pictured opposite (far left) in a promo picture session for the new guitar, clutching an early example. The other picture opposite shows McGuinn in 1990 presenting a rare white-finished 370/12RM to **Dave Stewart**, the ex-Eurythmics guitarist and, on this evidence, a keen fashion hound.

Buck says that with any electric 12-string it all comes down to tuning. He'll use a tuner to get his Rick 12 in tune – and then adjust it by ear. "Usually I'll flat the G-string, just a tiny bit, and I quite often flat the octave string on the low E, but not the regular E. Any time you go up on the G it's going to sound a little out of tune, so I try to go a little flat. That makes the chords ringy and gives you a little extra kind of harmonic thing. Half the time when you're doing an overdub with a 12 you have to stop half way through and retune."

In this way – and others – Buck considers his electric 12s as useful tools in the studio. Live, he's less keen, mostly because of the way those Gs will drift, but he often has a 620/12 to hand. Rickenbackers in general he rates highly for their on-the-road resilience. "I've had plenty of guitars where you just touch them, almost, and they dent. Ricks are strong: I don't have problems with wiring, the necks are super-sturdy, and they don't get bent. This makes sense – specially on the road 200 days of the year, like we were."

His long-term favourite, the black 360 six-string, was stolen after an R.E.M. gig in Finland in September 2008. Buck tells me it was an inside job. "They came back and said they wanted a million euros for it. We said: but we've offered $10,000 as a reward, with no questions asked. If you turn it in for that, you're a hero, you're the guy who found our guitar. On the other hand, if you ask for anything more, you're a blackmailer."

The thief had a think about that and came back with a counter-offer. "He said well, OK, how about $10,000 and you fix my mom's teeth? And we're like: what? It was just insanity. So we paid him the $10,000." Buck had to sign a contract that said he would not turn the thief in to the police. "So even if I decided to have someone follow the guy who picked up the money, find out who he was … I have a legally-binding contract saying that I can't pursue that. But I don't care – I wouldn't have done that anyway. On the other hand, if I met him in a bar, I probably would have, you know, beaten the shit out of him."

It's a nice thought. But it was a special moment for Buck to get back his beloved guitar. "I'm in the middle of a tour, and my entire rig, which I've been using for years, is designed for this guitar and maybe one other. I was having trouble getting any kind of real tone. So it was nice to have the Rickenbacker back and to just not have to think about it," he says with a sigh. "We have a lot of fans who come regularly to a lot of shows, and like 50 of them were holding up a sign that said 'Welcome Back Rickenbacker'. It was really sweet."[67]

Rickenbacker decided during the 80s to exploit its associations over the years with famous players. John Hall wanted to produce a guitar that offered something special, giving the potential customer the feeling that here was an instrument only a small number of people would be privileged to own. In a sense, the idea was to echo the feelings that many players have about vintage guitars – but in a brand new model. In short, Rickenbacker's plan was to produce limited-edition guitars.

However, after internal discussions and informal talks with retailers and distributors, Hall saw a more adventurous opportunity present itself, and he decided to make a line of 'signature model' artist-endorsed guitars. In itself this was not a new marketing concept.

The idea had been around for many years, at least since Gibson's Nick Lucas acoustic guitar of the late 20s. Virtually all modern guitar companies issue such signature models. But it was new for Rickenbacker, and the added marketing twist was to combine it with the attraction of a strictly limited production run.

Rickenbacker issued a numbered certificate with each of the limited-edition guitars, making it easier to control the quantity produced and emphasising to the customer that this was not merely a mass-produced guitar but an exclusive and collectable instrument.

At the time of writing, Rickenbacker has produced limited-edition signature guitars for eight artists. The Who's Pete Townshend was the first player to be so honoured, in 1987, and he was followed by Roger McGuinn (edition released 1988), John Kay (ex-Steppenwolf; also 1988), Susanna Hoffs (The Bangles; 1988), John Lennon (1989), Tom Petty (1991), Glenn Frey (ex-Eagles; 1992), and Carl Wilson (2000).

As we've learned, Townshend had used (and abused) some of Rickenbacker's f-hole export models in The Who's heyday during the mid 60s. Rickenbacker had already begun in 1987 to produce a non-vibrato reissue of the two-pickup Rose-Morris 1997 (335S) with export features such as f-hole and black control knobs. So it was logical to go one better for the Pete Townshend limited-edition model, and Rickenbacker settled on a three-pickup Rose-Morris 1998 (345S), but without the vibrato, which Townshend had never liked.

Rickenbacker made contact with Townshend through Trevor Smith and Linda Garson, who ran Rickenbacker's UK office, and stressed to him the artistic and historic value of such a project. The company explained that they wanted to make a limited run of the guitars, and this presented what to some musicians is another bonus: such a deal would not necessarily mean a long-term association.

Townshend was still identified in the minds of many pop fans with his habit in the 60s of smashing (primarily Rickenbacker) guitars on-stage. So it is likely that he was not alone in seeing the irony of a modern Rickenbacker Townshend model. "I'm quite surprised now that Rickenbacker are happy to have me sponsor an instrument which is so tied up with such an anarchic part of my career," he says. "But it's the only guitar I've ever sponsored … and I've done it partly out of guilt."[68]

Once all the details of the deal were complete, there came the problem of just how limited to make this first Rickenbacker limited edition. John Hall recalls the calculations. "We thought we were really stepping off the deep end by allowing 250 of the 1998PT Pete Townshend model to be produced – and they sold out in six weeks. Just like that! And of course," he laughs, "we then asked ourselves why on earth we hadn't gone with a thousand." Sales were indeed so rapid that the Townshend model was never featured in any of Rickenbacker's catalogues or pricelists of the period.

The next musician to be involved in Rickenbacker's new programme was Roger McGuinn. A 'rounded' new-style 370/12 appeared in 1988, limited to a more substantial edition of 1,000 guitars. McGuinn remembers: "When Rickenbacker's president John Hall called me to ask if I would be interested in participating in a limited-edition signature series, I was delighted. He asked what I wanted in my guitar. My first request was for an electronic compressor circuit to give my live performances the sound that we'd gotten on the Byrds records."

The circuit was primarily the work of Rickenbacker's engineer at the time, Bob Dessidaro, whom a colleague describes as being "very good at translating musicians' requirements into circuitry". John Hall says that it would have been useful to have had more time to spend on the circuit, especially in the area of conserving battery life. "But in the end we ran out of time, because we had to introduce the guitar at the trade show."[69]

The second item that McGuinn asked for on his signature guitar was a 12-saddle bridge, a unit conspicuous by its absence from any Rickenbacker 12-string before that. An ordinary six-saddle bridge on any 12-string will be a source of tuning problems for guitarists who expect to play higher than the first few frets. So Rickenbacker relented and, for the first time in nearly 25 years, installed a 12-saddle bridge on a 12-string guitar. To begin with, that was the only model on which it was available, but after the 370/12RM limited edition sold out during 1989, Rickenbacker began fitting it to other 12-string models. By 2009, it was a welcome feature of the 381/12V69 and the 660/12.

The pickguard on the Pete Townshend model had featured a logo of Townshend in classic arm-stretched windmilling pose. At first, Rickenbacker looked for a similar identifying logo for Roger McGuinn. One suggestion was a pair of small 'granny' sunglasses, as worn by McGuinn at the time of The Byrds. But a suitable image could not be found in time, and the guitar ended up with McGuinn's signature as the only adornment to the pickguard. As a nice personal touch, McGuinn signed all 1,000 of the certificates that went out with his limited-edition 370/12RM guitars.

McGuinn was clearly pleased with his signature guitar. "Rickenbacker's staff came up with an amazing circuit that sounded exactly like those early recordings. I loved it so much that I began using that circuit in the studio on my most recent work instead of the more costly studio compressors," he said a few years later. "Rickenbacker did a fine job on my signature model and sold the entire run of a thousand of them within a year. I'm very happy about the way the guitar turned out."[70]

McGuinn was not alone in his praise for the instrument. Customers for the 370/12RM included George Harrison, Pete Townshend, Tom Petty, David Crosby, Peter Buck, Johnny Marr (ex-The Smiths), and Dave Stewart (ex-Eurythmics).

McGuinn later put in a good word for a compressor in a pedal, the JangleBox, made by a company in Virginia. The aim was simple: to provide the smooth sound of compression in a box specially tailored and simplified for guitarists, so that players wouldn't have to lug around studio models made by Urei or (for the millionaire musician) Fairchild. "It's clean and quiet and it sounds very close to the built-in one I have in the 370/12RM," says McGuinn.[71]

John Kay, the ex-Steppenwolf guitarist, was the next choice for Rickenbacker's limited-edition programme. Kay had some ideas on what he wanted to incorporate into a guitar, notably a system of active electronics, and these details were worked out between Kay and Rickenbacker engineer Bob Dessidaro. Kay, who is colour-blind, specified the guitar's black and silver finish. His signature guitar had the highly carved body of the 381-style models, but with more modern electronics and new pickups.

"The guitar is based on the model 381 which I first played in 1968 and used on various Steppenwolf records," Kay wrote in the guitar's publicity material. He explained that the guitar incorporated humbucking pickups, active electronics, and phase switching. Rickenbacker managed to fit the two coils of the humbucking pickups into the same-size casing as traditional single-coil units. Kay concluded: "In these times of stamped-out imitations, it is truly a pleasure to be associated with something genuine and of high quality." The 381JK was launched in 1988.

Rickenbacker began discussions in 1987 with Susanna Hoffs of The Bangles about a signature guitar. She already played a 325 and said she'd like a 325-style body but with a full-scale neck, like the recent 350 Liverpool, and all in white. Rickenbacker had it in mind to make a guitar that also incorporated some of the more contemporary features that musicians had been requesting from the company, such as a pickup layout of two single-coils and a humbucker.

Brian Carman (who worked for Rickenbacker from 1965 to 1974 and 1984 to 1993) and Dick Burke built the white Hoffs guitar by hand, taking several months. Derek Davis, vice president at Rickenbacker from 1986 to 1991, remembers taking the finished item to show to Hoffs. "She said oh yes, she really liked it … but could we make it in black? It was totally the opposite of what we'd been working on! So we did the next one much quicker," he recalls, "and the limited edition came out in 1988 in black, with checker binding.

"To be honest, there was some resistance from heavy metal guys who didn't really want to play a guitar with a woman's name on it," says Davis. "But I think that when people found out what we were trying to do with the guitar, with the pickups and the slightly wider neck, they figured it was an interesting instrument."[72]

A couple more musicians who started using electric 12-strings in the 80s reflect the diversity of sounds that the instrument offers. Jim Babjak, guitarist of The Smithereens, leaned on a 60s sound with his Rickenbacker 330/12 for some of the group's finer cuts, including 'Elaine' on *Green Thoughts* (1988), 'Baby Be Good' on *11* (1989), or 'Now And Then' from *Blow Up* (1991).

Babjak's first 12-string had been a black Rickenbacker 360/12, which he bought in March 1980 at Manny's store on 48th Street in New York City. "I remember saving my unemployment cheques till I had enough money to buy it," he laughs. "It was one of the worst financial times in my life – and yet I still went out and purchased a Rickenbacker 12-string guitar. We'd just formed The Smithereens and were about to play our first show. I thought I'd be cool if I played one. It wasn't a very popular guitar then, as far as I could tell. I don't remember any other bands in our circuit using them during that period."

Babjak remembers a worrying moment on TV with another Rick 12. The Smithereens were about to play their latest single, 'Too Much Passion', on *The Tonight Show With Jay Leno* in 1991. "I'd recorded it with the 330/12," says Babjak, "but we were in the middle of a tour and I didn't have it with me, so I had ordered a 660/12 to use on the show. It was delivered to the TV studio before I got there, and I was really excited to try out this new guitar on national television.

"Our guitar tech, Chopper, pulled me aside when I arrived at the studio and told me not to be upset." Babjak knew right away that Chopper had lived up to his nickname. "The 660/12 was already on a stand and it looked beautiful. Then, Chopper pointed to where a chunk of wood was missing on the back of the neck. He'd dropped it while taking it out of its case. At least it didn't affect the intonation and was just an aesthetic issue. I … just laughed it off."

And for the listener who thinks he has good ears, Babjak offers a sonic clue to another 12-soaked Smithereens track, 'House We Used To Live In' on the *Green Thoughts* album. The attractive solo is electric 12-string – or at least most of it is. "I couldn't make a whole-step bend on the G-string in the second position on the Rick, because there was too much tension," Babjak explains. "So I overdubbed two tracks, playing a Stratocaster in octaves, and punched it in just for the bend. You can't really tell unless you know it's there."[73]

On the other side of the spectrum is Robin Guthrie, who in the 80s was responsible for the sound of The Cocteau Twins. His widescreen constructions make good use of assorted guitar textures, from six-string basses to 12-string acoustics and electrics, brought to life by everything his studio rack could offer and setting the scene for Liz Fraser's remarkable voice. "It's different types of paintbrush," explains Guthrie, who today is a French resident and still happily making records, for the past dozen years or so in his own name.

"I don't think I've made a record where I've not pulled out a 12-string," he says. "For chimey stuff, there's nothing quite like it. One of the tricks is the open-tuned 12-string, so that you get as many open strings droning away as possible. I love that sound. You drop the E-string down to D, you leave the B, the G, the D, and you drop the A down to G and pull the lowest E up to G. With just a few shapes, two or three fingers at the most, you can run up and down the neck. I've used that extensively – to the extent that it's getting a bit tedious now."

Guthrie's favourite is a white Fender Electric XII he's had since about 1984, when it replaced a Vox Phantom XII. "I've tried Rickenbackers, and I find them a nightmare. They just hurt my fingers a lot."

The danger is to overdo 12-string, he reckons. "At the time when I used to run it through all my effects and things, I don't think I'd ever considered or even heard a 12-string in that way. Not that I was the first to put it through a pedal, but at that point I'd never heard those sounds before. So I was really happy to use them. But there weren't really any songs where the rhythm parts were 12-string and the melodies were 12-string, or vice versa – I think it was one or the other. Otherwise it's like too much of a good thing."

Electric 12 remains an important part of Guthrie's sound kit for current projects. "Maybe not in quite such an energetic way, perhaps, but certainly in terms of overdubs and melodies," he says. "Different brushes, like I said. But the 12-string sound is such a big sparkle, and I'm always quite taken with it."[74]

Meanwhile, over at Rickenbacker, the company's 1988 pricelist featured 24 electric guitars under three headings. *Guitars*: 230 Hamburg $499, 250 El Dorado $669; 610 $599; 610/12 $699; 620 $699; 620/12 $799; 320 $869; 330 $899; 330/12 $999; 350 Liverpool $979; 360 $999; 360WB $1,099; 360/12 $1,099; 360/12WB $1,199; 362/12 special-order double-neck $2,599.

Vintage Reissues: 325V59 $1,299; 325V63 $1,299; 1997 $1,099; 1997VB $1,149; 381V69 $1,599; 381/12V69 $1,749.

Limited Editions: 350SH Susanna Hoffs $1,279; 370/12RME1 Roger McGuinn $1,399; 381JK John Kay $1,699.

In January 1989, the company moved its guitar factory from Kilson Drive, after some 27 years at that site, and consolidated factory and offices at the present building on the corner of South Main and Stevens in Santa Ana. The flow of products through the plant was immediately improved, the facilities for paint spraying in particular were upgraded, and in general the new factory became a more suitable manufacturing environment. By the early 90s, on another upward sales curve, Rickenbacker had some 75 people working at the factory, but this was down again to about 60 in 1994. By 2009, it was up around 85.

Later in 1989, the company issued a special group of limited-edition models relating to one of the company's most famous players, John Lennon. Rickenbacker made contact with Yoko Ono through her attorney. Derek Davis negotiated on behalf of Rickenbacker and pointed out that the company wanted to make an authentic tribute to John Lennon. "We said that from a musical instrument manufacturer's point of view, we would be as sensitive to John Lennon as he was to his music – and that was very sincere, that wasn't bullshit. Anyway, her attorney called back and said yes, they wanted to talk about it."[75]

After the go-ahead, the team at Rickenbacker did some detailed research. John Hall recalls that there was much debate about the exact shape of the headstock. "We found and borrowed a 325 in Los Angeles that was within a few serial numbers of John Lennon's 1964 model. At the factory, we had a whole stack of tooling for the head, and we just went through the stack until we matched it."

Rickenbacker realised that the task involved was much more than merely issuing a 325 with John Lennon's name on it. Accordingly, the team accumulated a large collection of reference material relating to Lennon's instrument, and after much thought and discussion they came up with the 325JL, which one insider referred to at the time as "the most authentic representation of the guitar that John Lennon played".

As well as the 'correct' short-scale 325, there was also a full-scale version of the limited edition, called model 355JL, and a full-scale 12-string, the 355/12JL, prompted by a custom 325/12 they'd made for country guitarist John Jorgenson, best known for his work

● **Pete Townshend** was the first musician to be honoured with a Rickenbacker signature model, introduced in 1987 as a limited run of just 250 guitars. Pete is pictured wth the **1998PT** (above) and a fine example is shown (right), complete with windmilling Pete logo. **Susanna Hoffs** of The Bangles (below) was a big Rick fan, and her 1988 signature model was the **350SH**.

● Rickenbacker launched its series of **John Lennon** signature models in 1989; three are pictured together (right). They are the **325JL** (bottom), which reproduces the 325 that Rick made for Lennon in 1964, and a long-scale version, the **355JL** (top left), without vibrato. There was also a 355JLVB, with vibrato. Last of the trio here is the **355/12JL** – a fine example is also pictured, left – a long-scale version of the 320/12 that Lennon was given but rarely used. Another 80s limited edition was the **381JK**, named for the Steppenwolf guitarist **John Kay**. An example is pictured (bottom) and in a 1988 promo shot (right).

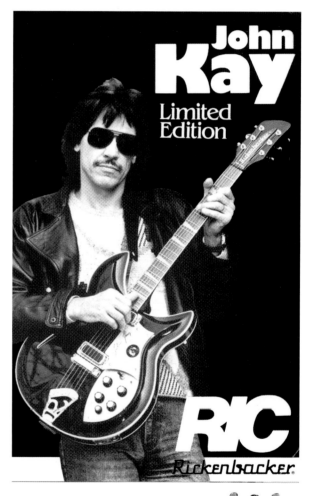

in The Desert Rose Band, The Hellecasters, and with Elton John's band. (A production 325/12 appeared in briefly in 1985.) Rickenbacker's John Lennon limited edition of 2,000 guitars therefore consisted of short-scale, full-scale vibrato and non-vibrato, and full-scale 12-string versions.

Yoko Ono was very particular about the way in which Lennon's image was interpreted, and she insisted Rickenbacker use an artist's impression rather than a photograph of him in advertising and promotional material. The logo on the guitar was a Lennon self-portrait, the same as that used in the movie *Imagine* released around the same time as the guitars. The launch of the Lennon models gave Rickenbacker a great deal of publicity across the media, and these guitars did more to raise general awareness of Rickenbacker's instruments than perhaps any other recent model the company has produced, with the possible exception of the McGuinn signature model.

Tom Petty & The Heartbreakers had long championed the Rickenbacker cause, and an official association with Petty and the group's lead guitarist Mike Campbell began in 1987, when informal discussions were opened about custom guitars for the two Californian musicians. Dick Burke and Brian Carman subsequently built Petty an unusual solid maple old-style 360. This fulfilled Petty's desire for a six-string that looked like the 12-string George Harrison played, as well as one that would not feed back, as the semi-acoustics were prone to do. The disadvantage for Petty was of course its weight.

Around 1990, Petty began to talk to Rickenbacker about a solidbody 600-style 12-string as a potential instrument for the company's limited-edition programme. He had been associated with the 'cresting wave' shape of this family of solidbody Rickenbackers since he appeared on the cover of the group's successful *Damn The Torpedoes* album in 1979 with Mike Campbell's 620/12.

"They approached me about doing a signature model, and they wanted to use the solidbody one," Petty recalls. "So I said OK, here's what I'd do. I would make the neck a little bit wider, because in the old ones, when you get down near the end, it can be really hard to fit all your fingers in. I had them expand the neck just a little bit and it made it a lot nicer."

The 660/12TP was launched at the NAMM trade show in 1991, a handsome guitar constructed from selected bird's-eye maple. It had checkered binding around the edge of the body, as requested by Petty, as well as that wider neck. One of the most common criticisms of Rickenbacker's 12-string instruments is that for many guitarists the neck is too narrow, especially at the nut, and that the strings consequently feel too close together. "I think they made about a thousand," says Petty, "and then they just took my name off and kept making them, you know?" Petty is referring to the continuation of his model in the Rickenbacker line from 1999 as the 660/12. (Rickenbacker did a similar thing with the Lennon 355/12JL, continuing it from 1994 as the 350/12V63.)

"I went to see Bruce Springsteen playing on *Saturday Night Live*," says Petty, "and there was one in the dressing room. He says, is this yours? I said yeah, hey, I designed this. And he said you're kidding. I said look, it's got the wide neck. That's my thing – they just took my name off it. He said to me wow, we got two of 'em. I said well, there's two royalties I didn't get."

Petty is still a big Rickenbacker fan. He reports that the first decent electric he had was a 330 six-string, bought in the 60s, and one of his favourite six-strings that he uses all the time is the 360 that Rickenbacker made him in the late 80s. His first electric 12 was a Vox Phantom, but he wanted a Rickenbacker. Finally he got a mapleglo (natural) 360/12 in 1980, from dealer Norm's Rare Guitars.

His favourite 12 today is a 1964 Rose-Morris 1993 that he got a few years back – it's the one he used at the Superbowl show that The Heartbreakers played in 2008. "I actually got the receipt and everything – someone had bought it originally from a shop in Liverpool. It sounds like an organ, almost, so deep and rich. Some of them can be kind of thin, but this one is very rich. I've started playing it more and more."

Heartbreakers guitarist Mike Campbell was another early convert to the Rick 12 sound. "I wanted either a George Harrison type or a Roger McGuinn type, the large body. I was in California and we were working on our first album. We didn't have an electric 12-string in the band and I really wanted one. *Recycler* was like a precursor to eBay – it was a magazine where people could advertise stuff for sale. You'd call someone up and go over to their house and make a deal."

Campbell looked in the *Recycler* one day, probably around 1975, and there was an ad for a Rickenbacker 12-string at $200. He took the two-hour drive out to Anaheim, trying to contain his excitement. "The guy brought it out, and it's actually the guitar you see on the cover of *Damn The Torpedoes*, that small solidbody Rickenbacker. When he opened it up my heart sank: this is the little one! I wanted the big one! I said this is not really what I want."

Campbell gave it a play and took a punt: he offered the guy $120. And walked out with the 620/12. He had no idea of its significance in the history of electric 12-string guitars. "Years later, we made a couple of trips to the Rickenbacker factory, and they said, do you realise that this guitar was the next one off the assembly line after George's? By some stroke of luck I had a really vintage one that was right in the same ilk as his, even though it was small-body."

Remarkably, the Rick that Campbell bought on that day was the third one of the experimental trio of electric 12s that Rickenbacker produced in 1963. Campbell immediately put it to use and played it on a lot of Heartbreakers records. "And on tour," he says proudly. "That was our 12-string for quite a while. It's a great little guitar. But I don't take it on the road now, because it's so valuable. I've been offered quite a lot of money for it, beyond what I paid for it – which is kind of funny. A bit more than $120, yes." Rickenbacker offered a production 620/12 from 1981.

Petty got his mapleglo 360/12 in 1980, and around the middle of that decade Campbell bought a mapleglo '64 rounded-edge 360/12. The two tell me about some of the

● **Tom Petty** has been a fan of Rickenbackers since he bought a 330 in the 60s, but when it came time for a Petty signature model, it had to be a 12. The **660/12TP** (example pictured below, and with Petty, left) was introduced in 1991. Each guitar of the edition of 1,000 included checker body binding, a 12-saddle brdge, and, crucially, a wider neck – good for players who find Rick's regular 12-string spacing too narrow. Petty has played other 12s, too, including a **360/12** (right). When he appeared on 1979's **Damn The Torpedoes** (opposite) with Mike Campbell's 620/12, it caused a leap in popularity for Rick 12s. Meanwhile, Rickenbacker forged ahead with its **vintage reissue** programme, featured in a 1995 **catalogue** (far right).

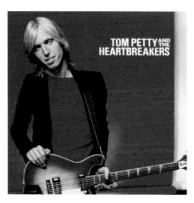

● Mike Campbell. lead guitarist with The Heartbreakers, bought this 1963 **620/12** (main guitar, below) in the mid 70s. It was his first Rick 12, but he had no idea that it was only the second 12-string Rickenbacker had ever made. Petty posed with it on the **Damn The Torpedoes** jacket (above) and Campbell still plays it – pictured (right) in 1985.

group's records with electric 12 – and there are some real treasures. It might sound like there's a 12 on 'American Girl' but it's octaves on a six-string. "You've probably heard the story," says Campbell. "When we finally got to meet Roger McGuinn, he said he'd heard that on the radio and thought it was him. He was with his manager, and turned and said, 'When did I do that?' The manager says, that's not you. He thought it was something he'd recorded and forgotten about. And so then he wanted to meet us."

I ask Petty for his favourite 12 moment, and it's hard to disagree with his choice, which comes from the band's 1981 LP *Hard Promises*. "It's 'The Waiting' – that's a very 12-string intro, and it's the one that really sticks out," he says. "I knew right off that's what I would use for it. Electric 12s are maybe not as noticed when you use them in the rhythm, but they can make a beautiful colour in there."

If you like your guitarists tasteful, thoughtful, and playing for the song, then Campbell's work will always make you smile. As for his 12-string highlights, there's 'Listen To Her Heart' on the second album, 1978's *You're Gonna Get It*, "a signature Beatles-type Rickenbacker 12-string riff" as he aptly describes his 620/12 part. "When we got to the solo, I wanted a melody that was similar to what Tom was singing. I found it on the B-string, up high, and then by accident or chance or accidental genius, I don't know what, I realised that if I let the E-string underneath it ring along too, it sounded twice as beautiful and twice as full."

It's a classic example, says Campbell, of how the nature of the electric 12 can lead you to a technique. "I found out later, talking to Roger McGuinn, that he does that. George Harrison said he and Roger had talked about it, too, how on a lot of Byrds stuff – say 'Turn! Turn! Turn!' – the melody will be on the G-string. You're just sliding up and down on the G-string, with the E and B underneath ringing open against that melody note. That is a really beautiful and stirring technique, so chimey and mysterious."

We should also mention the lovely deep 12 statement from Petty and his blond 360/12 on the solo of 'Flirting With Time' from his solo record *Highway Companion*. Campbell, meanwhile, has a rarity to share, which he played on that same guitar. "There's a song you may not know called 'Waiting For Tonight', I think a B-side, when we had The Bangles sing background. It's me playing Tom's 12-string, and it's very nice, very Byrdsy – very Roger McGuinn."

Petty says that he finds Rick 12s effortless to play. "I've tried all sorts, and none of them chime quite like a Rickenbacker. There's just something to the sound of it that you're not going to get out of the others. Fender made a really nice 12-string, but it just doesn't chime the same. It doesn't look nearly as good, either. I have a double-neck Rick twelve-and-six that I've used in the studio at times. It makes this really wild sound – with such a big body on it, it really rings out. But it's impossible to play it live, because it's just the heaviest thing in the world. I tried it once and went, OK, enough of that."[76]

Campbell, like many Rick 12-string players, has experienced the cramped chord effect. That's when you find there's not enough space at the nut end of the board to play your usual chords. Ever the optimist, he says this forces you to find new voicings, mini versions of the familiar shapes – and that too can help you stumble on new ideas.

"I've learned a lot of things on the guitar because it was a 12-string and it forced my mind to look for different intervals, or different things that ring right," he says. "And the Rickenbackers are really delicate. If you're holding one and you lean on it, it will kind of go out of tune. You have to cradle it lightly and not lean – unless you want it to swoop or something. You have to be very careful. You have to put on your thinking cap and focus, or it will sound really horrible."[77]

At Rickenbacker, John Hall's wife Cindalee became president of Rickenbacker International Corporation in 1990. Meanwhile, John devised a new line of Rickenbackers, the 24-fret 650 series. Launched in 1992, they shared the body style of the earlier 400 and 600 'cresting wave' series, but with their wider necks and high output pickups, the 650s were designed to compete with mainstream instruments. "We've always been criticised at Rickenbacker for 'only making rhythm guitars'," says Hall. "Well, these are lead guitars, and that's precisely how we're marketing them."[78]

Also that year, Hall restyled the 230 Hamburg and 250 El Dorado guitars, renaming them as the 220 Hamburg and the 260 El Dorado and giving them slightly wider, satin-finished necks, contouring on the body, a more conventional control circuit, and the humbucking pickups developed for the John Kay model. A version of the revised Hamburg model provided Rickenbacker with another limited-edition model, the 230GF Glenn Frey, derived from what seemed to be the rather basic requirements of the ex-Eagles musician. All the 200-series models were gone from the line by 1996.

Some good pop bands showcased Rickenbacker electric 12s in the 90s, including U2 on 'Even Better Than The Real Thing', a single from *Achtung Baby* (1991) with Edge playing his 330/12; The Mavericks using a Rick 360/12 on 'What A Crying Shame' (album title track, 1994); and The Rembrandts with a 450/12 on 'I'll Be There For You' (a 1995 hit single, better known as the *Friends* TV theme).

Forty years after its first two 'modern' electric models appeared, Rickenbacker's 1994 pricelist featured 37 electric guitars, separated into three headings. *Guitars*: 220 Hamburg $899; 260 El Dorado $1,049; 610 $999; 610/12 $1,099; 620 $1,099; 620/12 $1,199; 650 Atlantis $1,099; 650 Colorado $1,099; 650 Dakota $999; 650 Excalibur $1,199; 650 Sierra $1,099; 330 $1,199; 330/12 $1,299; 340 $1,324; 340/12 $1,424; 350 Liverpool $1,269; 360 $1,319; 360WB $1,429; 360/12 $1,419; 360/12WB $1,529; 370 $1,444; 370WB $1,554; 370/12 $1,544; 370/12WB $1,654.

Limited Editions: 230 Glenn Frey $999; 381 John Kay $1,799; 660/12 Tom Petty $1,699.

Vintage Reissues: 325V59 $1,659; 325V63 $1,659; 350V63 $1,689; 350/12V63 $1,789; 360V64 $1,559; 360/12V64 $1,659; 1997 $1,429; 1997SPC $1,554; 381V69 $2,189; 381/12V69 $2,289.

In the meantime, Rickenbacker began talking to ex-Beach Boy Carl Wilson about a signature model in the late 90s. They made a prototype – but nothing like the limited edition that eventually appeared in 2000. It was a black 260-shape solidbody six-string with humbuckers and vibrato and plenty of checkerboard binding. "That was where we were headed," recalls John Hall "Then, Carl was in my office one day talking about it, and he said, you know I haven't been feeling real good lately, my back hurts." Wilson headed off to the doctor. "And that was the day he learned he had cancer."

Wilson died in February 1998 at the age of just 52. Rickenbacker's Carl Wilson model came together through musician Billy Hinsche, whose sister was Carl's wife. "Billy shepherded that project," says Hall, "going with the wishes of Carl's two sons, Jonah and Justyn, and they came up with something different. They went back to a version of the guitar that Carl had used in the 60s." The results that appeared in 2000 were the 360CW and the 360/12CW, based on 1965-era rounded-body models and limited to 500 each. A portion of the proceeds went to the Carl Wilson Foundation, which helps fund cancer research and assist those with the disease.

As we near the end of our story, it's worth reminding ourselves that electric 12-string does not necessarily mean Rickenbacker. "In dollars and cents," says Hall, "the 12-string is not particularly important to Rickenbacker. It's a small part. However, we still have about a 98 percent share of the world market in electric 12-strings. It's a segment that we totally dominate, but it isn't a huge segment."[79]

We've seen and heard about electric 12s from Fender and Gibson and Danelectro and Vox and Burns and Epiphone and others, and those makers' guitars still provide an alternative for some musicians. One such is Nels Cline, a Los Angeles-born guitarist who at the time of writing plays with the Chicago-based band Wilco.

If your ears are attuned to new sounds and you're interested in the more exploratory side of guitar playing, you'll know Cline's own records, too, which are full of an inquisitive, improvising nature, as is his work alongside fellow adventurers such as Thurston Moore of Sonic Youth. In Wilco, he's bringing some new layers of sound and imagination to an already impressive band.

Cline's musical inspiration around the age of ten was The Byrds, so as a budding guitarist he soon got a Rickenbacker 12 – but that one didn't last long, thanks to some unwise storage decisions. As a professional, Cline has been through quite a few guitars, and while you'll mostly hear him today using his favoured Fender Jazzmaster, his electric-12 mainstay is a Jerry Jones Neptune. Jones is a Nashville-based maker who interprets old Danelectro designs for a line of modern instruments.

"My friend G.E. Simpson, a guitar player with whom I still play sometimes, told me about Jerry Jones guitars," says Cline. "He had one of Jerry's first 12-strings, around 1997, and I thought they were so great. I'd bought one of Jerry's baritone guitars, and it's one of the greatest guitars I own, just for sheer sustain."

Cline got a Jones Danelectro-style 12, which he used on tour with The Geraldine Fibbers in the 90s. When he joined Jeff Tweedy's Wilco in 2004, he wanted something fresh. "The Neptune was less slavishly like a Danelectro, and with the three lipstick-case pickups it really all came together – you can get some beautiful tones with those. I'm sort of a slave to three pickups on a 12-string."

On his own records, listen out for electric 12 on pieces such as 'Ghost Of The Pinata' on the 2002 album *Instrumentals* by The Nels Cline Singers, or 'The Luxury Of Silk' on The Nels Cline Trio's *Sad* (1998). You can hear Cline playing his Neptune 12-string with Wilco on 'I Am Trying To Break Your Heart' and 'Heavy Metal Drummer' from *Kicking Television: Live In Chicago* (2005), 'You Are My Face' from *Sky Blue Sky* (2007), and 'You And I' from 2009's *Wilco (the album)*.

"There's 12 on the flipped solo at the end of 'You and I'," says Cline. "It's my obvious tribute to The Byrds' *Younger Than Yesterday* album. One of the early things that Jeff Tweedy and I were bonding on was our love of The Byrds. Anybody who plays in an American rock'n'roll band and who doesn't love The Byrds is probably kidding themselves. I'm not trying to be doctrinaire – but for me it's so pivotal."

He's found inspiration among other 12-string players, too, especially the acoustic open-tunings of Ralph Towner (solo records, or with Weather Report and Oregon), and marks out for attention Pat Metheny's ES-335-12 work on 'Sirabhorn' from 1975's *Bright Sized Life* and Jimmy Bryant's remarkable Stratosphere double-neck playing in the 50s. But The Byrds clearly made a mark.

"I saw them in Central Park in 1967, the first big show I ever got to go see," Cline recalls. "McGuinn was amazing, and I thought it was the greatest thing ever. Man, that sound was the best. I was about 12; I'm 53 now. It was psychedelia and folk-rock and soul. It destroyed me for life! Absolute listening magic for a young boy – it was a wondrous sound that has never worn off."[80]

Rickenbacker made a small change to the headstock of some 12-string models in 2005. On the non-replica and non-vintage models, the 'slots' in the headstock were now cut all the way through, where before they were routed channels. This takes out a little weight – usually a good thing tonally in the head of a guitar – and apparently makes the guitar easier to string. "Our guys down on the shop floor who are stringing guitars all day think it's the greatest thing we ever did," laughs Hall.[81]

Rickenbacker has introduced very few new models in recent years. The 380L Laguna, launched in 1996, was a pretty, pickguard-less 300-series guitar with oiled walnut body, gold hardware, and dot markers on a maple fingerboard, while the model 1996 was a reissue, available in 2006 only, based on the old Rose-Morris-style 325.

There have been a few renamings: the 660/12TP Tom Petty became simply the 660/12 in 1999, and a 'new' matching six-string was derived from it at the same time, the 660. The 650 series had some name changes and lost a few models. A striking pale blue finish harking back to some specials made in the 50s for Jim Reeves's band provided the Blue Boy finish for a few models, at first only for non-US markets, in 2002. There was also a renaming of some of the vintage models, with a C series introduced in 2001 alongside the V models amid some name changes.

"It's a frustration," says Hall. "I'd love to do some new models – and indeed we have developed some – but there is no manufacturing capacity to support them. It's just about impossible to put out anything new given our two-year backlog." This was the position at Rickenbacker at the time of writing, in 2009. "We've had this kind of backlog now for 12, 13 years," says Hall, "and so it makes no sense to do new models."[82]

Many players today use electric 12-strings, for all the reasons we've come upon in this book and no doubt a few more too. Johnny Marr likes to remind himself occasionally that the guitar is a machine. Some of his best 12-string work was with The Smiths back in the 80s, but since then he's made some fine records with Electronic, The The, Talking Heads, The Healers, Kirsty MacColl, The Cribs, and others. Throughout his eclectic and engaging work, acoustic and electric 12s are never far away. But a machine? What can he mean?

"For me, anything that stops you taking the guitar for granted and reminds you that it's not a piece of sporting equipment is important," says Marr. "I think the 12-string particularly does that, because of the effort it takes to re-string it, particularly a Rickenbacker. There's a lot of moving pieces on it. You have to be aware of its engineering aspects and approach it like a machine to make music."

Guitar players, like anyone else, prefer things to be easy. "And that means you can become a bit of an automaton and stop using your ears. And then the next thing you know you're complaining that you're uninspired. I like anything that snaps you out of your complacency. And 12-strings can do that. They take some thinking about, but you do get used to them."

For a while in The Smiths, Marr had to live with a nickname: jingle-jangle Johnny. When success came early in the band's recording career, many people began to say Marr's sound was like The Byrds. "Up until that point, I knew a fair bit about The Byrds, but I wasn't trying to ape them by any means. So I went back and got into them and investigated. That was when that term started to be used, which I've never been able to entirely shake off. Actually, I don't mind it so much now – I quite like it."

It was fair and unfair at the same time. One of The Smiths' best-known songs was 'How Soon Is Now', and there's not a jingle or a jangle anywhere near it. More like an unspellable eeeeowww. But when it comes to 'This Charming Man', even if it was made on Telecaster and Rick six-string, the result is jingle plus jangle squared. "Now I think about it," says Marr, "I really asked for it."

What is worthy of the nickname? He earmarks 'The Headmaster Ritual' from 1985's *Meat Is Murder* album, in an open D tuning with a capo on the second fret, where he merges Martin D-28 acoustic 12-string, Rickenbacker six, and Les Paul six. "With all those big open strings ringing out, on a clean sound, with harmonies and capos, it's just like harmonic crazy," says Marr. "And if you play like I do, where I'm constantly searching for little melodies inside what you're doing, it will ring out in a big way."

Marr also mentions 'Stop Me If You Think You've Heard This One Before' from *Strangeways Here We Come* (1987) as another peak of jangle. "You hear my Rickenbacker 12 most clearly on the intro, but the song was built on electric 12-string – I wrote it on that guitar. On the instrumental B-side 'The Draize Train', again you can hear a Rick 12 very clearly on the intro."

The Smiths appeared at a time when many young guitarists were casting off old assumptions about what you could and couldn't do with your instrument. Not just rock assumptions, but punk too. "My feeling, being around 17, 18, was that as much as I loved a lot of punk records, to me it wasn't the letter A in a new alphabet – it was the letter Z in the old one. People using Les Pauls; still playing with distorted sounds; using barre chords; essentially Chuck Berry. Done very well, and I particularly loved Iggy & The Stooges, and anyone of my age group loved the Pistols. But after that, it felt a little bit like a clean slate."

One opportunity that presented itself was to play funky and clean. He mentions Orange Juice and Wire and Talking Heads in this area. Marr himself went the other way. "I sped the right hand up quite a lot, and to fill out that sound with no sustain I ended up using a lot of arpeggios and doing a lot of strumming. I was picking a lot to fill out the sound – because my band were never really going to be playing funky James Brown things. I realise now that all of that went into my choice of Rickenbacker."

Marr went out and bought a new Rickenbacker 330 six-string as soon as the band got their first publishing deal, to replace his Gretsch Super Axe. "I wanted it to bring out a side of me that I was keen to explore: more chordal and melodic; essentially being a songwriter. Most singers like chord changes, and you tend not to be too modal on a Rickenbacker – it encourages chord progressions and harmonic changes and arpeggios and all those things."

As for electric 12, he'd borrowed a Rickenbacker 12 from Roxy Music's Phil Manzanera for The Smiths' appearance on chart show *Top Of The Pops* for 'This Charming Man' (which is probably why some think, erroneously, that there's 12-string on the record). Then he got his own, at first in 1986 an ex-John Entwistle Rose-Morris model 1993, followed by a black McGuinn signature model in 1999.

The first Smiths album has Rick 12 on 'Suffer Little Children', and then subsequently, Marr says, he began to use it more and more – for example on 'Big Mouth Strikes Again' and 'Never Had No One Ever' on *The Queen Is Dead* (1986), and generally on the group's last album, *Strangeways Here We Come* (1987). "That record has the most amount of 12-string, and it's often a sunburst Gibson ES-335-12, which I later gave to Bernard Butler. You hear it on the start of 'Paint A Vulgar Picture' and it was on 'Sheila Take A Bow' and 'I Started Something'."

Since The Smiths, Marr has used 12-strings for drama and richness in a number of settings. 'Get The Message' by Electronic (1991) is one of his favourites, a track built around his Martin and Rickenbacker 12-strings. Kirsty MacColl's 'Tread Lightly', from her album *Kite* (1989), had a lot of 12, and it marked the start of Marr's concerted use of effects, especially delay.

"*Kite* wasn't my record," he says, "even though I was very involved in it, I play on most of it, and I wrote some of it. When it's my record, I can spend several hours layering up

● At the time of writing, the last new Rickenbacker 12-string model was the 2000 limited edition **360/12CW Carl Wilson** (main guitar), based on a 60s instrument that the Beach Boys guitarist played. Sadly, Wilson died in 1998 before the project was completed.

● The electric 12-string continues to attract musicians with an ear for the unusual. **Nels Cline** with Wilco (below left) plays a Jerry Jones Neptune, while the ex-Smiths guitarist **Johnny Marr** is pictured (below) in 2006 playing his Rickenbacker 370/12 McGuinn model 12-string with The Healers.

● And so we near the end of the book – but a story that continues for Rickenbacker and for the electric 12-string, even as you read this. In 2006, Rickenbacker marked 75 years since the historic Frying Pan electric with four instruments that had a special **anniversary logo** (above). Those decades since have marked strong progress for the brand and its most important guitar, the electric 12-string. Players like **Ed O'Brien** of Radiohead (pictured above in 2008 with 360/12) find inspiration in the 12's harmonic complexity, the way it points to melodic invention, and the sheer musical pleasure that 12 chiming strings can bring in that strange place beyond six.

things, but when it's someone else's, and I want to get an effect, I don't think it's too cool to say OK, can I put guitar number nine on now? So when I wanted to get big things moving around, I started to get more effective with delays."

Another key record for his 12-string work is 'You Are The Magic' by Johnny Marr & The Healers from their album *Boomslang* (2003). By then, Marr also had a Rickenbacker McGuinn signature 12, which he'd pulled back to an 11-string, removing the octave string from the G pair. He found this helped the clarity and intonation of that string for soloing and improved the overall sound of the guitar. For the Healers 'Magic' track, Marr developed his way of combining acoustic and electric 12-strings, something that had its seeds in the Smiths track 'Please Please Please Let Me Get What I Want'.

"On 'Magic' I run the 12-string clean through a Fender Deluxe, so it sounds like a hot acoustic, and throughout the track it gets hotter and hotter," Marr explains. "That's the sound I really like and come back to more and more. I find with those gentle intros that the 12-string acoustic isn't enough on its own, but the electric if it's amped up can be too much – so I end up getting a compromise between the two of them. It's a sound that's pleasing to me, that cross between an electric and an acoustic."

The lure of the 12-string remains constant for Marr. But he knows that not everyone recognises the value of the instrument. "You have to apply yourself to play electric 12-string, and especially Rickenbacker," he says. "In a sense, you have to apply yourself constantly to tune it, depending on what sort of condition the guitar's in. There are plenty of things that a rock guitar player can't do readily on a 12-string – and I think that's one of the benefits of the instrument, because it stops you going into those automatic clichés.

"One of the reasons I played a Rickenbacker six-string in the early days of The Smiths was to shut down some of the roads that you have as a guitar player that make you play without thinking," says Marr. "And that's why I play a Jaguar now. You just can't be unthinkingly bluesy on it. You have to approach it as something you're going to get guitar music out of – and if you want to be bluesy or rocky, you have to be really deliberate about it. All those things about the electric 12 – the tuning, the physical application, the no-entry signs – will put some guitar players off. But what might be considered limitations by some people are for me an opening to play in a certain way."[83]

Meanwhile in the instrument industry, there were accusations that Rickenbacker had manipulated the market to keep demand and prices high by limiting production. To Rickenbacker boss John Hall, these seemed ridiculous – why miss out on business? "We try to think outside the box," he says. "We don't generally look to what the rest of the industry are doing."

John has now been at Rickenbacker longer than his father: F.C. Hall was there from the company's formation in 1953 until 1984; John started part-time in 1966, full-time in 1969. Now he is CEO. "There is a cult following, a very strong brand loyalty," says Hall. "It seems that our customers can't just buy one – a typical Rickenbacker owner has about five Ricks. Rather extraordinary."

Rickenbacker fans clearly love Rickenbacker, and in part it's because of the company's willingness to beat its own path. "It could be because we're just crazy, too," says Hall, smiling. "All I can say is the proof is in the pudding. We have a long backlog of orders. And a lot of people don't realise that the guitar business is only a fairly small part of our overall business. The company today is still quite active in real-estate development and oil production, and that has been the case for quite a long time. Those enterprises have done pretty well."

How important is the fact that Rickenbackers are still US-made in a world of increasing competition from makers around the world? "That's been a basic premise of the company," says Hall. "There's no reason to make our guitars elsewhere and there's no reason to knock ourselves off somewhere else."

The only thing that has changed, says Hall, is that the company sources some components overseas. That's primarily because some components just aren't made in the US any more. "Nobody makes pots or capacitors here now. The big American companies like CTS that used to make pots, for example, first moved to Mexico and now to Taiwan. That's where all of the best pots come from. But I would never consider the guitars being made anywhere else."[84]

Rickenbacker's 2009 pricelist grouped a modest 15 electric guitars under three headings. Almost half of them are 12-string models.

Guitars: 620 $1,829; 620/12 $2,209; 650 Colorado $1,829; 660 $2,649; 660/12 $3,109; 330 $1,999; 330/12 $2,459; 360 $2,499; 360/12 $2,939; 370/12 $3,129.

C Series: 325C64 Miami $3,599; 360/12C63 $3,839.

Vintage Reissues: 350V63 $3,059; 381V69 $4,949; 381/12V69 $5,409.

Alongside the specific reissues, the Rickenbacker line today offers instruments with strong roots in the best guitars of its past. The newer end is covered with that single 650, but the heart of the modern Rick line is the 300-series, which includes three 12-strings: the 330/12 (mono, two pickups, dot markers), the360/12 (stereo, two pickups, triangle markers), and the 370/12 (stereo, three pickups, triangle markers), and has a six-string to match the 330 and 360.

It's easy to imagine that without F.C. Hall's far-sighted gifts back in the 60s to John Lennon and, especially, George Harrison, Rickenbacker's history might have been very different – and this would have been a much shorter book.

Instead, Rickenbacker continues to attract new players and their new musical ideas to an apparently timeless set of designs and sounds. As Harrison once said: "The Rickenbacker 12-string sound is a sound on its own."[85]

Footnotes

1 *Concise History Of The Frying Pan* (BBC Radio 1, 1987)
2 *Melody Maker* April 4 1963
3 *Concise History Of The Frying Pan* (BBC Radio 1, 1987)
4 A. Rickenbacher *The History Of Rickenbacker* (unpublished, June 1960)
5 Brozman *National Resonator Instruments*
6 A. Rickenbacher *The History Of Rickenbacker* (unpublished, June 1960)
7 *Guitar Player* April 1974
8 *Guitar Player* April 1974
9 Unpublished interview with John Hall, circa 1968
10 A. Rickenbacher *The History Of Rickenbacker* (unpublished, June 1960)
11 A. Rickenbacher *The History Of Rickenbacker* (unpublished, June 1960)
12 Author's interview November 16 1993
13 Author's interview October 27 1992
14 Author's interview November 17 1993
15 Author's interview February 10 1992
16 Author's interview November 16 1993
17 Author's interview November 17 1993
18 *Beat Instrumental* December 1964
19 *Concise History Of The Frying Pan* (BBC Radio 1, 1987)
20 Author's interview August 18 1994
21 Author's interview August 18 1994
22 *Concise History Of The Frying Pan* (BBC Radio 1, 1987)
23 Author's interview August 10 2009
24 Author's interview July 29 2009
25 Tulloch *Neptune Bound*
26 Author's interview November 17 1993
27 Author's interview April 20 1994
28 Author's interview November 16 1993
29 Author's interview November 16 1993
30 *Concise History Of The Frying Pan* (BBC Radio 1, 1987)
31 Author's interview November 16 1993
32 *Beat Instrumental* November 1964
33 *Melody Maker* March 21 1964
34 *Melody Maker* April 4 1963
35 Author's interview August 13 2009
36 Lewisohn *Complete Beatles Recording Sessions*
37 Emerick *Here, There And Everywhere*
38 Author's interview July 16 2009
39 Author's interview June 10 2009
40 *Concise History Of The Frying Pan* (BBC Radio 1, 1987)
41 Author's interview November 17 1993
42 Author's interview November 16 1993
43 Author's interview November 17 1993
44 Author's interview July 31 2009
45 *Goldmine* September 6 1991
46 Author's interview July 23 2009
47 Author's interview April 16 1994
48 *Guitar Player* October 2004
49 *Premier Guitar* November 2008
50 Author's interview April 16 1994
51 *Ear Candy* April 1999
52 *Modern Guitars* February 15 2006
53 *Concise History Of The Frying Pan* (BBC Radio 1, 1987)
54 *Guitar World* October 2002
55 Author's interview August 4 2009
56 Author's interview June 22 2009
57 Author's interview April 13 1994
58 Author's interview April 14 1994
59 Author's interview September 16 2009
60 Author's interview April 14 1994
61 Author's interview June 26 2009
62 Author's interview April 16 1994
63 Author's interview July 23 2009
64 Author's interview July 24 2009
65 Author's interview September 11 2009
66 Author's interview April 13 1994
67 Author's interview July 24 2009
68 *Concise History Of The Frying Pan* (BBC Radio 1, 1987)
69 Author's interview April 13 1994
70 Author's interview April 16 1994
71 *Premier Guitar* November 2008
72 Author's interview April 24 1994
73 Author's interview July 21 2009
74 Author's interview July 15 2009
75 Author's interview April 24 1994
76 Author's interview August 10 2009
77 Author's interview July 22 2009
78 Author's interview April 13 1994
79 Author's interview September 11 2009
80 Author's interview July 21 2009
81 Author's interview September 11 2009
82 Author's interview September 11 2009
83 Author's interview August 17 2009
84 Author's interview September 11 2009
85 *Concise History Of The Frying Pan* (BBC Radio 1, 1987)

MODEL DIRECTORY

The simple, condensed format of this model directory provides information about Rickenbacker's electric guitars through the years. The following notes are designed to help you use this unique directory. At the end of the directory is a dating guide and model chronology.

How to use the model directory

The directory covers all electric Spanish guitars (in other words, excluding lap steels) issued by Rickenbacker between August 1932 and August 2009. Each is allocated to one of 15 distinctive body shapes, which we've called Styles, and these are numbered in the chronological order of their introduction. Corresponding body silhouettes are ranged along the bottom of each page-spread to provide a useful visual reference. Under the Style headings, the relevant models are listed in numerical and/or alphabetical order.

At the head of each entry is the **model number** (and name if there is one) in bold type. Rickenbacker rarely puts a model number or name on the guitar itself. There are exceptions: some instruments have the model number on the truss-rod cover. Otherwise, we've drawn all the model names in this book from Rickenbacker's literature and pricelists, whether printed or online. Bear in mind that these sources often have occasional lapses in consistency, in content, and in the compiler's descriptive powers.

Following the model name is a **date or range of dates** showing the production period of the instrument (a 'c' in front of a date means circa, or about). These dates and any others in the model directory and the model chronology are as accurate as possible but should still be considered approximate. Like most guitar companies,

Rickenbacker has not always been concerned with providing a method to pinpoint the exact date of manufacture of a particular instrument. The dates here and in the dating guide later in this book should be regarded as just that: a guide, not gospel.

In italics, following the model number or name and production dates, is a brief **one-sentence identification** of the model in question. This concise summary of unique features is intended to help you recognise a specific model at a glance.

For some guitars there may be a sentence below this, reading "As ... except:". This refers to another model entry and describes any major differences between the two.

In most entries, there will be a **list of specification points**, separated into groups and providing details of the model's features. In the order listed, they refer to:

- Neck, fingerboard, position markers, scale-length, frets, headstock.
- Body, finish.
- Pickups.
- Controls, jack location.
- Pickguard.
- Bridge, tailpiece.
- Hardware finish.
- Special features, if any.

Not every model will need all eight points, and to avoid undue repetition we have considered a number of **features common to all** Rickenbacker electric guitars. They are:

- Unbound rosewood fingerboard unless stated.
- Full scale length 24¼ inches unless stated.

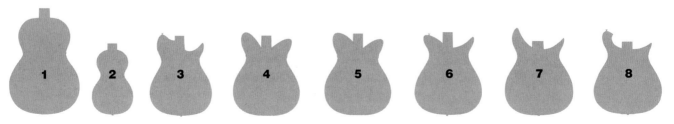

- Truss rod adjustment at headstock unless stated.
- Unbound body unless stated.
- Nickel or chrome-plated hardware unless stated.

Some models were made in a number of **variations**, and where applicable these are listed, in italics, after the specification points. Any other **general comments** are made here, too, also in italics.

Some entries only have a short listing, all in italics. This is usually because the model concerned is a reissue of or a re-creation based on an earlier guitar, and the text refers to the original instrument.

Alternative model numbers or names are listed as separate, brief italicised entries. They read "See …", cross-referring to a main listing.

All this information is designed to tell you more about your Rickenbacker guitar. By using the general information and illustrations earlier in the book and combining them with the knowledge collected in this reference section, you should be able to build up a full picture of your instrument and its pedigree.

Just before we get into the model directory, here are a few more points to bear in mind when you use this section of the book.

Production dates

Rickenbacker's pricelists sometimes show models going in and out of production across the years, perhaps ceasing and then reappearing later, and not always in the same guise. In reality, production was often more constant, usually through Special Orders. This facility allowed for a model no longer officially offered to nonetheless be obtained as a special order, usually by upgrading a still listed standard version – adding,

typically, a third pickup or a vibrato tailpiece.

Where we know this happens, we've combined the officially listed model and the special order version under one overall production span, with a suitable note. This results in extended and continuous periods of availability, which makes things easier to understand and, we feel, more accurately reflects Rickenbacker's production policy.

Optional features

Rickenbacker has often provided a varied menu of optional features available for special order. **Left-hand** versions are regularly offered and were available at the time of writing. **Right-handed stringing** on a lefty is a much more unusual variation – currently still offered but rarely encountered. **Slant Frets** were intended to offer improved comfort and playability, but the unusual visuals were enough to guarantee little demand.

Various **cosmetic choices** have been offered, such as custom colours and black and white checkered body binding. **Custom Trim** meant reversed colour choices of body binding and plastic components – black instead of standard white, or white instead of standard black. **Pickup options** have included medium, high, and very high gain units, including custom or vintage types. The option of a **third pickup** has been offered at various times for suitable models, usually when three-pickup versions are not officially listed. The option was dropped in 2007 and at the time of writing was not available.

The Vintage RIC **vibrato tailpiece** was the original Ac'cent unit, revived in 1985. Guitars with optional vibrato were usually offered when the official vibrato-equipped model was not listed. The option was dropped in 2007 and at the time of writing was not available.

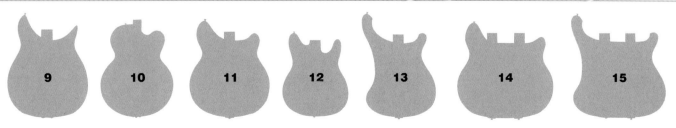

Pickguards

In late 1958, Rickenbacker replaced the single pickguard used on some models with a novel and distinctive two-piece unit. This new version stylishly combined a large base with a small separate upper section, raised on three spacers. We have called this a 'two-tier' pickguard throughout the book.

Soundholes

Most semi-acoustic models have a single soundhole, although it has sometimes been absent from the short scale 310/320 series. The soundhole is either a scimitar like 'slash' or one with the traditional 'f' shape. The f-hole was one of the features specified by UK importer Rose-Morris for its 60s export versions.

Shipping totals

Rickenbacker has asked us to point out that shipping totals previously published elsewhere are far from accurate. Those figures were apparently compiled from only a small selection of sales documents, with consequent errors in the yearly output and with the quantities quoted being significantly less than the actual numbers produced.

STYLE ONE

(1932–50)

Non-cutaway large body

ELECTRO SPANISH 1932–35 *F-holes in upper bouts of flat-top body.*
Style one
- Bound fingerboard, dot markers; 25-inch scale, 19 frets (14 to body); slotted headstock.
- Hollow flat-top bound body with small f-holes in upper bouts; sunburst.
- One horseshoe pickup at bridge.
- No controls (one volume control on body from c1934).
- Single-saddle wooden bridge, separate trapeze tailpiece.
Neck and body made by Harmony, Chicago.

KEN ROBERTS 1935–40 *F-holes in lower bouts of flat-top body.*
Style one
- Bound fingerboard, dot markers; 25-inch scale, 22 frets (17 to body).
- Hollow flat-top bound body with f-holes in lower bouts; sunburst.
- One horseshoe pickup at bridge.
- One control (volume) on body, side-mounted jack.
- Single-saddle bridge, separate vibrato tailpiece.
Neck and body made by Harmony, Chicago.

SP *See Spanish listing.*

SPANISH 1946–50 *F-holes in upper bouts of archtop body.*

Style one
- Bound fingerboard, block markers; 25-inch scale, 20 frets (14 to body).
- Hollow archtop bound body with small f-holes in upper bouts; sunburst.
- One horseshoe pickup at bridge.
- Two controls (volume, tone) on body, side-mounted jack.
- Single-saddle wooden bridge, separate trapeze tailpiece.
Neck and body made by Harmony, Chicago.
Also known as SP model.

S-59 1940–42 *F-holes in lower bouts of archtop body.*
Style one
- Alternate diamond and twin-dot

 1 2 3 4 5 6 7 8

markers; 25¾-inch scale, 19 frets
(14 to body).

- Hollow archtop bound body with f-holes in lower bouts; natural.
- One narrow horseshoe pickup on body-width bracket near bridge.
- One control (volume) and jack on pickup bracket.
- Single-saddle wooden bridge, separate trapeze tailpiece.

Neck and body made by Kay, Chicago.

STYLE TWO
(1935–42)
Non-cutaway small body

ELECTRO SPANISH 1935–42 *Very small black body with five chromed or white plates on front.*
Style two
- Bakelite neck; dot markers; 24 frets (14 to body).
- Bakelite slab body; black.
- One horseshoe pickup at bridge.
- One control (volume) on plate (two controls – volume, tone – on two plates from c1938), side-mounted jack.
- Five chrome-plated metal plates (white-painted from c1939) on body front.
- Single-saddle bridge/tailpiece; vibrato tailpiece option.

Known as Model B from c1940.

MODEL B *See Electro Spanish listing.*

VIBROLA SPANISH 1937–42 *Very small black body with four chromed plates on front.*
Style two
- Bakelite neck; dot markers; 24 frets (14 to body).
- Bakelite slab body; black.
- One horseshoe pickup at bridge.
- Two controls (volume, vibrato) on two plates, side-mounted jack.
- Four chrome-plated metal plates on body front.
- Single-saddle bridge, motorised vibrato tailpiece.

STYLE THREE
(1954–59)
Offset cutaways (left shallow, right deep) on small body

COMBO 600 1954–59 *Two controls and one selector.*
Style three
- Bolt-on or glued-in neck; dot markers; 20 frets (21 frets from c1957).
- Carved-top body; natural or colours.
- One horseshoe pickup at bridge.
- Two controls (volume, tone) and

three-way selector, all on body (all on elongated pickguard from c1956); side-mounted jack.
- Black plastic pickguard (black or gold plastic elongated pickguard from c1956).
- Single-saddle bridge/tailpiece with metal cover.

COMBO 800 1954–59 *Two controls and two selectors.*
Style three
- Bolt-on or glued-in neck; dot markers; 20 frets (21 frets from c1957).
- Carved-top body; natural or colours.
- One horseshoe double pickup at bridge (plus neck pickup from c1957).
- Two controls (volume, tone) and two three-way selectors, all on body (all on elongated pickguard from c1956); side-mounted jack.
- Black plastic pickguard (black or gold plastic elongated pickguard from c1956).
- Six-saddle bridge/tailpiece with metal cover.

STYLE FOUR
(1956–57)
Offset cutaways (both curving out; 'tulip' shape) on small body

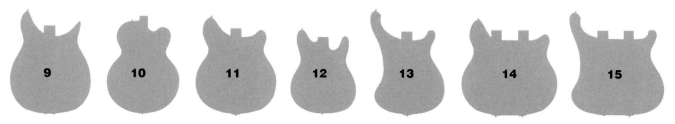

COMBO 400 1956–57 *One pickup at neck.*

Style four

■ Through-neck; dot markers; 21 frets.

■ Solid body; colours.

■ One pickup at neck.

■ Two controls (volume, tone), three-way selector, and jack, all on pickguard.

■ Anodised metal pickguard.

■ Single-saddle bridge/tailpiece with metal cover.

COMBO 450 1957 *Two pickups.*

Style four

■ Through-neck; dot markers; 21 frets.

■ Solid body; colours.

■ Two pickups.

■ Two controls (volume, tone), three-way selector, and jack, all on pickguard.

■ Anodised metal pickguard.

■ Single-saddle bridge/tailpiece with metal cover.

MODEL 1000 1957 *Short-scale neck, 18 frets, one pickup.*

Style four

■ Through-neck; dot markers; short-scale, 18 frets.

■ Solid body; colours.

■ One pickup near bridge.

■ Two controls (volume, tone), three-way selector, and jack, all on

pickguard.

■ Anodised metal pickguard.

■ Single-saddle bridge/tailpiece with metal cover.

STYLE FIVE
(1957)

Offset cutaways (both curving out, but thicker left horn; uneven 'tulip' shape) on small body

MODEL 900 1957 *Short-scale neck, one pickup.*

Style five

■ Through-neck; dot markers; short-scale, 21 frets.

■ Solid body; colours.

■ One pickup near bridge.

■ Two controls (volume, tone), three-way selector, and jack, all on pickguard.

■ Anodised metal pickguard.

■ Single-saddle bridge/tailpiece with metal cover.

MODEL 950 1957 *Short-scale neck, two pickups.*

Style five

■ Through-neck; dot markers; short-scale, 21 frets.

■ Solid body; colours.

■ Two pickups.

■ Two controls (volume, tone), three-

way selector, and jack, all on pickguard.

■ Anodised metal pickguard.

■ Single-saddle bridge/tailpiece with metal cover.

STYLE SIX
(1957–71)

Offset cutaways (left curving out, right shallow with slight inward curve) on small body

COMBO 400 1957–58 *One pickup at neck.*

Style six

■ Through-neck; dot markers; 21 frets.

■ Solid body; colours.

■ One pickup at neck.

■ Two controls (volume, tone), two three-way selectors, and jack, all on pickguard.

■ Anodised metal pickguard.

■ Single-saddle bridge/tailpiece with metal cover.

COMBO 450 1957–58 *Two pickups.*

Style six

■ Through-neck; dot markers; 21 frets.

■ Solid body; colours.

■ Two pickups.

■ Two controls (volume, tone), two three-way selectors, and jack, all on pickguard.

- Anodised metal pickguard.
- Single-saddle bridge/tailpiece with metal cover.

MODEL 900 1957–71 *Short-scale neck, one pickup near bridge.*
Style six

- Glued-in or through-neck; dot markers; short-scale, 21 frets.
- Solid body; colours.
- One pickup near bridge.
- Two controls (volume, tone), two three-way selectors, and jack, all on pickguard.
- Anodised metal pickguard.
- Single-saddle bridge/tailpiece with metal cover.

MODEL 950 1957–71 *Short-scale neck, two pickups.*
Style six

- Glued-in or through-neck; dot markers; short-scale, 21 frets.
- Solid body; colours.
- Two pickups.
- Two controls (volume, tone), two three-way selectors, and jack, all on pickguard.
- Anodised metal pickguard.
- Single-saddle bridge/tailpiece with metal cover.

MODEL 1000 1957–71 *Short-scale neck, 18 frets, one pickup near bridge.*

Style six

- Glued-in or through-neck; dot markers; short-scale, 18 frets.
- Solid body; colours.
- One pickup near bridge.
- Two controls (volume, tone), two three-way selectors, and jack, all on pickguard.
- Anodised metal pickguard.
- Single-saddle bridge/tailpiece with metal cover.

STYLE SEVEN
(1957–current)
Offset cutaways with pointed horns ('sweeping crescent' profile across both cutaways) on small body

COMBO 650 1957–59 *Two controls and one selector.*
Style seven

- Glued-in or through-neck; dot markers; 21 frets.
- Carved-top body; natural or colours.
- One horseshoe pickup at bridge.
- Two controls (volume, tone) and three-way selector, all on pickguard; side-mounted jack.
- Gold plastic pickguard.
- Six-saddle bridge/tailpiece with metal cover.

COMBO 850 1957–59 *Two controls*

and two selectors.
Style seven

- Glued-in or through-neck; dot markers; 21 frets.
- Carved-top body; natural or colours.
- One horseshoe double pickup at bridge (plus neck pickup from c1957).
- Two controls (volume, tone) and two three-way selectors, all on pickguard; side-mounted jack.
- Gold plastic pickguard.
- Six-saddle bridge/tailpiece with metal cover.

310 1958–77, 1981–84 *Short-scale neck, two pickups.*
Style seven

- Glued-in neck; dot markers; short-scale, 21 frets.
- Semi-acoustic body with or without one soundhole; sunburst, natural, or colours.
- Two pickups.
- Four controls (two volume, two tone; fifth 'blend' control added from c1963) and three-way selector, all on pickguard; side-mounted jack.
- Two-tier gold plastic pickguard (white plastic from c1963).
- Six-saddle bridge, separate tailpiece.

Earliest examples with two controls (volume, tone) and three-way selector on single gold plastic pickguard.

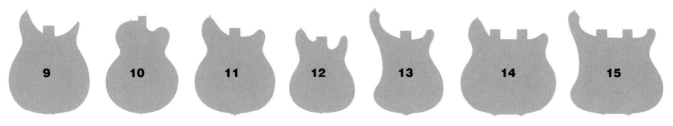

315 1958–75 *Short-scale neck, two pickups, vibrato tailpiece.*
Style seven
- Glued-in neck; dot markers; short-scale, 21 frets.
- Semi-acoustic body with or without one soundhole; sunburst, natural, or colours.
- Two pickups.
- Four controls (two volume, two tone; fifth 'blend' control added from c1963) and three-way selector, all on pickguard; side-mounted jack.
- Two-tier gold plastic pickguard (white plastic from c1963).
- Six-saddle bridge, separate vibrato tailpiece.
Earliest examples with two controls (volume, tone) and three-way selector on single gold plastic pickguard.

320 1958–1992 *Short-scale neck, three pickups.*
Style seven
- Glued-in neck; dot markers; short-scale, 21 frets.
- Semi-acoustic body with or without one soundhole; sunburst, natural, or colours.
- Three pickups.
- Four controls (two volume, two tone; fifth 'blend' control added from c1963) and three-way selector, all on pickguard; side-mounted jack.

- Two-tier gold plastic pickguard (white plastic from c1963).
- Six-saddle bridge, separate tailpiece.
Earliest examples with two controls (volume, tone) and three-way selector on single gold plastic pickguard. Known as 320 Liverpool 1985–87.

320B 1983–84 *Vintage reissue based on 1960-period four-knob original.*

320 LIVERPOOL *See 320 listing.*

320VB *See 325 listing.*

325 1958–75, 1985–92 *Short-scale neck, three pickups, vibrato tailpiece.*
Style seven
- Glued-in neck; dot markers; short-scale, 21 frets.
- Semi-acoustic body with or without one soundhole; sunburst, natural, or colours.
- Three pickups.
- Four controls (two volume, two tone; fifth 'blend' control added from c1963) and three-way selector, all on pickguard; side-mounted jack.
- Two-tier gold plastic pickguard (white plastic from c1963).
- Six-saddle bridge, separate vibrato tailpiece.
Earliest examples with two controls

(volume, tone) and three-way selector on single gold plastic pickguard.
325S export version known as Model 1996 in UK 1964–67.
Available as 320VB (320 with vibrato tailpiece option, thus 325 specification) from 1985.

325B 1983–84 *Vintage reissue based on 1960-period four knob original.*

325C58 HAMBURG 2001–08 *Vintage reissue based on 1958-period four-knob original. Renamed version of 325V59.*

325C64 MIAMI 2001–current *Vintage reissue based on 1964-period five-knob original. Renamed version of 325V63.*

325JL JOHN LENNON 1989–93 *Signature on pickguard, short-scale, vibrato tailpiece.*
Style seven
- Glued-in neck; dot markers; short-scale, 21 frets.
- Semi-acoustic body; black only.
- Three pickups.
- Five controls (two volume, two tone, one blend) and three-way selector, all on pickguard; side-mounted jack.
- Two-tier white plastic pickguard.
- Six-saddle bridge, separate vibrato tailpiece.

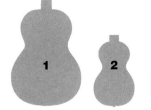 1
 2
 3
 4
 5
 6
 7
8

John Lennon signature, 'Limited Edition', and Lennon drawing on pickguard.
Limited edition of 974, including 21 left-hand examples.

325S *See 325 listing*

325V59 HAMBURG 1984–2000
Vintage reissue based on 1959-period four-knob original. Hamburg name added c1996. Renamed 325C58 Hamburg in 2001.

325V63 MIAMI 1984–2000 *Vintage reissue based on 1963-period five-knob original. Miami name added c1996. Renamed 325C64 Miami in 2001.*

325/12 1985–86 *12 strings, short-scale neck, three pickups.*
Style seven
- Glued-in neck; dot markers; short-scale, 21 frets; 12-string headstock.
- Semi-acoustic body with or without one soundhole; sunburst, natural, or colours.
- Three pickups.
- Five controls (two volume, two tone, one blend) and three-way selector, all on pickguard; side-mounted jack.
- Two-tier white plastic pickguard.
- Six-saddle bridge, separate tailpiece.

This ought logically to have been named a 320/12, as it has no vibrato.

350 LIVERPOOL 1983–95 *24 frets, three pickups.*
Style seven
- Glued-in neck; dot markers; 24 frets.
- Semi-acoustic body with no soundhole; sunburst, natural, or colours.
- Three pickups.
- Five controls (two volume, two tone, one blend) and three-way selector, all on pickguard; side-mounted jack.
- Two-tier white plastic pickguard.
- Six-saddle bridge, separate tailpiece.

350SH SUSANNA HOFFS 1988–90 *24 frets, signature on pickguard.*
Style seven
- Glued-in neck with bound fingerboard, triangle markers; 24 frets.
- Semi-acoustic bound body; black only.
- Three pickups, humbucker at bridge.
- Five controls (two volume, two tone, one blend) and three-way selector, all on pickguard; side-mounted jack.
- Two-tier white plastic pickguard.
- Six-saddle bridge, separate tailpiece.

Susanna Hoffs signature and 'Limited Edition' on pickguard.
Limited edition of 250, including 4 left-hand examples.

350VB *See 355 Liverpool Plus listing.*

350V63 LIVERPOOL 1994 current
Signature-less version of 355JL John Lennon, discontinued in 1993. Liverpool name added c1996.

350/12V63 LIVERPOOL 12
1994–2007 *Signature-less version of 355/12JL John Lennon 12-string, discontinued in 1993. Liverpool 12 name added c1996.*

355 LIVERPOOL PLUS 1983–85 *24 frets, three pickups, vibrato tailpiece.*
Style seven
- Glued-in neck; dot markers; 24 frets.
- Semi-acoustic body with no sound-hole; sunburst, natural, or colours
- Three pickups.
- Five controls (two volume, two tone, one blend) and three-way selector, all on pickguard; side-mounted jack.
- Two-tier white plastic pickguard.
- Six-saddle bridge, separate vibrato tailpiece.
Renamed 350VB (350 with vibrato tailpiece option, thus 355 specification) 1985 only.

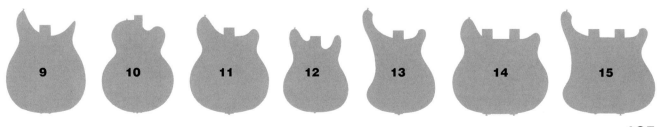

355JL JOHN LENNON 1989–93

Signature on pickguard, full-scale, non-vibrato tailpiece.

Style seven

■ Glued-in neck; dot markers; 21 frets.

■ Semi-acoustic body; black only.

■ Three pickups.

■ Five controls (two volume, two tone, one blend) and three-way selector, all on pickguard; side-mounted jack.

■ Two-tier white plastic pickguard.

■ Six-saddle bridge, separate tailpiece.

■ John Lennon signature, 'Limited Edition', and Lennon drawing on pickguard.

Limited edition of 668, including 8 left-hand examples.

This ought logically to have been named a 350, as it has no vibrato.

355JLVB JOHN LENNON 1989–93

Signature on pickguard, full-scale, vibrato tailpiece.

As 355JL, except:

■ Vibrato tailpiece.

Limited edition of 23.

355/12JL JOHN LENNON 1989–93

12 strings, signature on pickguard.

Style seven

■ Glued-in neck; dot markers; 21 frets; 12-string headstock.

■ Semi-acoustic body; black only.

■ Three pickups.

■ Five controls (two volume, two tone, one blend) and three-way selector, all on pickguard; side-mounted jack.

■ Two-tier white plastic pickguard.

■ Six-saddle bridge, separate tailpiece.

■ John Lennon signature, 'Limited Edition', and Lennon drawing on pickguard.

Limited edition of 334, including 5 left-hand examples.

This ought logically to have been named a 350/12, as it has no vibrato.

1996 *See 325 listing.*

1996 2007 *Vintage reissue based on the 1964-period export version of the 325.*

STYLE EIGHT
(1958–current)

Offset cutaways (with hooked left horn; 'cresting wave' profile across both cutaways) on small body

420 1965–83 *Dot markers, one pickup, large single pickguard.*

Style eight

■ Glued-in or through-neck; dot markers; 21 frets.

■ Solid body; sunburst, natural, or colours.

■ One pickup at bridge.

■ Two controls (volume, tone), three-way selector, and jack, all on pickguard.

■ White plastic pickguard.

Single-saddle bridge/tailpiece.

Renamed non-vibrato version of 425.

425 1958–72 *Dot markers, one pickup, large single pickguard.*

Style eight

■ Glued-in or through-neck; dot markers; 21 frets.

■ Solid body; sunburst, natural, or colours.

■ One pickup at bridge.

■ Two controls (volume, tone), three-way selector, and jack, all on pickguard.

■ White plastic pickguard.

■ Single-saddle bridge/tailpiece (vibrato tailpiece from 1965).

Until 1965, this broke with Rickenbacker tradition of --5 model numbers indicating a vibrato-equipped instrument. From that year, it gained a vibrato, while the non-vibrato version became the 'new' 420.

450 1958–85 *Dot markers, two pickups, large single pickguard.*

Style eight

■ Glued-in or through-neck; dot markers; 21 frets.

■ Solid body; sunburst, natural, colours.

■ Two pickups.

■ Four controls (two volume, two tone), three-way selector, and jack, all on pickguard.

■ Anodised metal pickguard (white plastic from c1962).

■ Six-saddle bridge/tailpiece with metal cover (single-saddle bridge/tailpiece from c1964).

Earliest examples with two controls (volume, tone) and two three-way selectors. Three-pickup versions exist.

450/12 1964–85 *12 strings, dot markers, two pickups, large single pickguard.*
Style eight

■ Through-neck; dot markers; 21 frets; 12-string headstock.

■ Solid body; sunburst, natural, or colours.

■ Two pickups.

■ Four controls (two volume, two tone), three-way selector, and jack, all on pickguard.

■ White plastic pickguard.

■ Single-saddle bridge/tailpiece.

456/12 1966–75 *12 strings, two pickups, 12/6-string converter unit.*
As 450/12, except:

■ 12/6-string converter unit mounted on body.

460 1961–85 *Triangle markers, two pickups, large single pickguard.*
Style eight

■ Through-neck with bound fingerboard, triangle markers; 21 frets.

■ Solid bound body; sunburst, natural, or colours.

■ Two pickups.

■ Five controls (two volume, two tone, one blend) and three-way selector, all on pickguard; side-mounted jack(s).

■ Anodised metal pickguard (white plastic from c1962).

■ Six-saddle bridge/tailpiece with metal cover (single-saddle bridge/tailpiece from c1964).

610 1985–95 *Dot markers, two pickups, two-tier pickguard.*
Style eight

■ Through-neck; dot markers; 21 frets.

■ Solid body; sunburst, natural, or colours.

■ Two pickups.

■ Five controls (two volume, two tone, blend) and three-way selector, all on pickguard; side-mounted jack.

■ Two-tier white plastic pickguard.

■ Six-saddle bridge, separate tailpiece.

610VB See 615 listing.

610/12 1988–95 *12 strings, dot markers, two pickups, two-tier pickguard.*
Style eight

■ Through-neck; dot markers; 21 frets; 12-string headstock.

■ Solid body; sunburst, natural, or colours.

■ Two pickups.

■ Five controls (two volume, two tone, blend) and three-way selector, all on pickguard; side-mounted jack.

■ Two-tier white plastic pickguard.

■ Six-saddle bridge, separate tailpiece.

615 1962–74, 1985 *Dot markers, two pickups, two-tier pickguard, vibrato tailpiece.*
Style eight

■ Through-neck; dot markers; 21 frets.

■ Solid body; sunburst, natural, or colours.

■ Two pickups.

■ Four controls (two volume, two tone; fifth 'blend' control added from c1963) and three-way selector, all on pickguard; side-mounted jack.

■ Two-tier white plastic pickguard.

■ Six-saddle bridge, separate vibrato tailpiece.

Earliest examples with gold plastic pickguard.
615S export version known as Model 1995 in UK 1964.

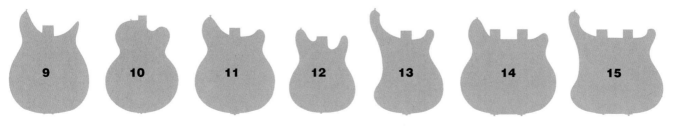

9   10   11   12   13   14   15

Available as 610VB (610 with vibrato tailpiece option, thus 615 specification) in 1985.

615S *See 615 listing.*

620 1974–current *Triangle markers, two pickups, two-tier pickguard.*
Style eight
- Through-neck with bound fingerboard, triangle markers, 21 frets.
- Solid bound body; sunburst, natural, or colours.
- Two pickups.
- Five controls (two volume, two tone, one blend) and three-way selector, all on pickguard; side-mounted jacks.
- Two-tier white plastic pickguard.
- Six-saddle bridge, separate tailpiece.

620VB *See 625 listing.*

620/12 1981–current *12 strings, triangle markers, two pickups, two-tier pickguard.*
Style eight
- Through-neck with bound fingerboard, triangle markers, 21 frets; 12-string headstock.
- Solid bound body; sunburst, natural, or colours.

- Two pickups.
- Five controls (two volume, two tone, one blend) and three-way selector, all on pickguard; side-mounted jacks.
- Two-tier white plastic pickguard.
- Six-saddle bridge, separate tailpiece.

625 1962–74, 1985 *Triangle markers, two pickups, two-tier pickguard, vibrato tailpiece.*
Style eight
- Through-neck with bound fingerboard, triangle markers, 21 frets.
- Solid bound body; sunburst, natural, or colours.
- Two pickups.
- Five controls (two volume, two tone, one blend) and three-way selector, all on pickguard; side-mounted jacks.
- Two-tier white plastic pickguard.
- Six-saddle bridge, separate vibrato tailpiece.
Available as 620VB (620 with vibrato tailpiece option, thus 625 specification) in 1985.

650A ATLANTIS 1992–2002 *Maple through-neck, 24 frets, blue body wings, chrome-plated hardware.*
Style eight

- All-maple through-neck; dot markers; 24 frets.
- Solid body; blue maple wings.
- Two pickups.
- Four controls (two volume, two tone) and three-way selector, all on pickguard; side-mounted jack.
- Chrome-plated metal pickguard.
- Six-saddle bridge, through-body stringing; vibrato option from 1994.

650C COLORADO 1993–current
Maple through-neck, 24 frets, all-black body, chrome-plated hardware.
As 650A Atlantis, except:
- Black body, neck, and headstock.

650D DAKOTA 1993–2007 *Maple through neck, 24 frets, walnut brown body wings, chrome-plated hardware.*
As 650A Atlantis, except:
- Headstock laminated with contrasting wood (walnut).
- Natural walnut wings.
- Oiled satin finish.

650E EXCALIBUR 1991–95 *Maple through-neck, 24 frets, vermilion brown body wings, gold-plated hardware.*
As 650A Atlantis, except:
- Headstock laminated with contrasting wood (vermilion).
- Natural vermilion wings.
- Gold-plated hardware.

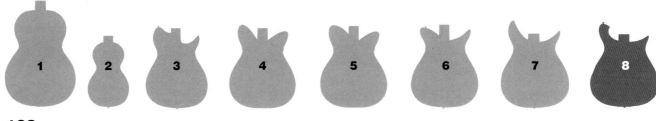

Renamed 650F Frisco in 1995.

650F FRISCO 1995–2002 *Renamed version of 650E Excalibur.*

650S SIERRA 1993–2007 *Maple through-neck, 24 frets, dark walnut brown body wings, gold-plated hardware.*
As 650A Atlantis, except:
- Headstock laminated with contrasting wood (dark walnut).
- Natural dark walnut wings.
- Gold-plated hardware.
- Oiled satin finish.

660 1999–current *Triangle markers, two pickups, two-tier gold plastic pickguard.*
Style eight
- Through-neck with bound fingerboard, triangle markers.
- Solid bound body; sunburst, natural, or colours.
- Two pickups.
- Five controls (two volume, two tone, blend) and three-way selector, all on pickguard; side-mounted jack.
- Two-tier gold plastic pickguard.
- Six-saddle bridge, separate flat trapeze tailpiece.

660/12 1999–current *12 strings, triangle markers, two pickups, two-tier gold plastic pickguard.*

As 660/12TP Tom Petty, except:
- No signature or 'Limited Edition' on pickguard.

660/12TP TOM PETTY 1991–96 *12 strings, triangle markers, signature on pickguard.*
Style eight
- Through-neck with bound fingerboard, triangle markers.
- Solid bound body; sunburst or black.
- Two pickups.
- Five controls (two volume, two tone, blend) and three-way selector, all on pickguard; side-mounted jack.
- Two-tier gold plastic pickguard.
- 12-saddle bridge, separate flat trapeze tailpiece.
- Tom Petty signature and 'Limited Edition' on pickguard.
Limited edition of 1,000, including 7 left-hand examples.

900 1971–79 *Short-scale neck, one pickup, large single pickguard.*
Style eight
- Glued-in neck; dot markers; short-scale, 21 frets.
- Solid body; sunburst, natural, or colours.
- One pickup.
- Two controls (volume, tone), three-way selector, and jack, all on pickguard.

- White plastic pickguard.
- Single-saddle bridge/tailpiece.

950 1971–79 *Short-scale neck, two pickups, large single pickguard.*
Style eight
- Glued-in neck; dot markers; short-scale, 21 frets.
- Solid body; sunburst, natural, or colours.
- Two pickups.
- Four controls (two volume, two tone), three-way selector, and jack, all on pickguard.
- White plastic pickguard.
- Single-saddle bridge/tailpiece.

1995 *See 615 listing.*

STYLE NINE
(1958–current)
Offset cutaways (with pointed horns; 'sweeping crescent' profile across both cutaways) on large body – often known as the 'sharp edge' or 'pointed' big-body style

330 1958–current *Dot markers, two pickups.*
Style nine
- Glued-in neck; dot markers; 21 frets (24 frets phased in from c1969).
- Semi-acoustic body with one

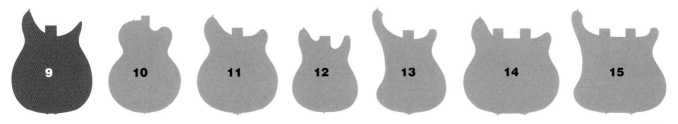

soundhole; sunburst, natural, or colours.

■ Two pickups.

■ Four controls (two volume, two tone; fifth 'blend' control added from c1963) and three-way selector, all on pickguard; side-mounted jack.

■ Two-tier gold plastic pickguard (white plastic from c1963).

■ Six-saddle bridge, separate tailpiece.

Earliest examples with two controls (volume, tone) and one or two three-way selectors on single gold plastic pickguard.

330VB *See 335 listing.*

330/12 1965–current *12 strings, dot markers, two pickups.*
Style nine

■ Glued-in neck; dot markers; 21 frets (24 frets phased in from c1969); 12-string headstock.

■ Semi-acoustic body with one soundhole; sunburst, natural, or colours.

■ Two pickups.

■ Five controls (two volume, two tone, one blend) and three-way selector, all on pickguard; side-mounted jack.

■ Two-tier white plastic pickguard.

■ Six-saddle bridge, separate tailpiece.

330S/12 export version known as Model 1993 in UK 1964–67.

330S/12 *See 330/12 listing.*

330VB *See 335 listing.*

331 1970–76 *Translucent plastic body front displaying the body's internal lighting.*
Style nine

■ Glued-in neck with bound fingerboard, dot markers; 24 frets.

■ Semi-acoustic body with translucent plastic sectioned front.

■ Two pickups.

■ Six controls (two volume, two tone, one blend, one light dimmer) and three-way selector, all on body front.

■ Six-saddle bridge, separate tailpiece.

■ Internal lights and circuitry, external power supply.

Earliest examples use straight rows of white lights fitted with coloured filters; later versions have staggered, coloured lights.

331/12 1970–75 *12 strings, translucent plastic body front displaying the body's internal lighting.*
As 331, except:

■ 12-string headstock.

335 1958–77, 1985–2007 *Dot markers, two pickups, vibrato tailpiece.*
Style nine

■ Glued-in neck; dot markers; 21 frets (24 frets phased in from c1969).

■ Semi-acoustic body with one soundhole; sunburst, natural, or colours.

■ Two pickups.

■ Four controls (two volume, two tone; fifth 'blend' control added from c1963) and three-way selector, all on pickguard; side-mounted jack.

■ Two-tier gold plastic pickguard (white plastic from c1963).

■ Six-saddle bridge, separate vibrato tailpiece.

Earliest examples with two controls (volume, tone) and one or two three-way selectors on single gold plastic pickguard.
335S export version known as Model 1997 in UK 1964–68.
Available as 330VB (330 with vibrato tailpiece option, thus 335 specification) from 1985.

335S *See 335 listing.*

336/12 1966–76 *12 strings, two pickups, 12/6-string converter unit.*
As 330/12, except:

■ 12/6-string converter unit mounted on body.

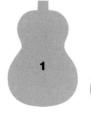

1   2   3   4   5   6   7   8

336S/12 export version known as Model 3262 in UK 1967.

336S/12 *See 336/12 listing.*

340 1958–2007 *Dot markers, three pickups.*
Style nine
- Glued-in neck; dot markers; 21 frets (24 frets phased in from c1969).
- Semi-acoustic body with one soundhole; sunburst, natural, or colours.
- Three pickups.
- Four controls (two volume, two tone; fifth 'blend' control added from c1963) and three-way selector, all on pickguard; side-mounted jack.
- Two-tier gold plastic pickguard (white plastic from c1963).
- Six-saddle bridge, separate tailpiece.

Earliest examples with two controls (volume, tone) and one or two three-way selectors on single gold plastic pickguard.

340VB *See 345 listing.*

340/12 1980–2007 *12 strings, dot markers, three pickups.*
Style nine
- Glued-in neck; dot markers; 24 frets; 12-string headstock.

- Semi-acoustic body with one soundhole; sunburst, natural, or colours.
- Three pickups.
- Five controls (two volume, two tone, one blend) and three-way selector, all on pickguard; side-mounted jack.
- Two-tier white plastic pickguard.
- Six-saddle bridge, separate tailpiece.

345 1958–75, 1985–2007 *Dot markers, three pickups, vibrato tailpiece.*
Style nine
- Glued-in neck; dot markers; 21 frets (24 frets phased in from c1969).
- Semi-acoustic body with one soundhole; sunburst, natural, or colours.
- Three pickups.
- Four controls (two volume, two tone; fifth 'blend' control added from c1963) and three-way selector, all on pickguard; side-mounted jack.
- Two-tier gold plastic pickguard (white plastic from c1963).
- Six-saddle bridge, separate vibrato tailpiece.

Earliest examples with two controls (volume, tone) and one or two three-way selectors on single gold plastic pickguard.
345S export version known as Model 1998 in UK 1964–67.
Available as 340VB (340 with vibrato

tailpiece option, thus 345 specification) from 1985.

345S *See 345 listing.*

360 1958–1995 *Triangle markers, two pickups.*
Style nine
- Glued-in neck with bound fingerboard, triangle markers; 21 frets (24 frets phased in from c1969).
- Semi-acoustic bound body with one soundhole; sunburst, natural, or colours.
- Two pickups.
- Four controls (two volume, two tone; fifth 'blend' control added from c1963) and three-way selector, all on pickguard; side-mounted jack(s).
- Two-tier gold plastic pickguard (white plastic from c1963).
- Six-saddle bridge, separate tailpiece.

Earliest examples with two controls (volume, tone) and one or two three-way selectors on single gold plastic pickguard.
SO (Special Order) examples available 1964–84.
Known from c1984 as 360WB, meaning 'with binding' on body front edge, in contrast to 360 in Style Eleven, which has no binding on front body edge.

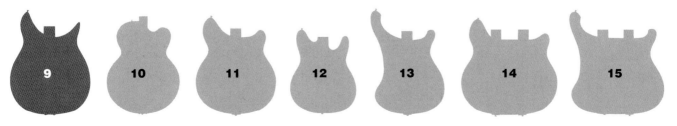

360V64 1991–2000 *Vintage reissue based on 1964-period original.*

360WB *See 360 listing, 370 listing.*

360WBVB *See 365 listing.*

360/12 1964–95 *12 strings, triangle markers, two pickups.*
Style nine
- Glued-in neck with bound fingerboard, triangle markers; 21 frets (24 frets phased in from c1969); 12-string headstock.
- Semi-acoustic bound body with one soundhole; sunburst, natural, or colours.
- Two pickups.
- Five controls (two volume, two tone, one blend) and three-way selector, all on pickguard; side-mounted jacks.
- Two-tier white plastic pickguard.
- Six-saddle bridge, separate tailpiece.
Known from 1964 as 360/12OS, meaning 'old style' body with front binding, later changed to 360/12WBBS, meaning 'white binding both sides', until c1984.
Known from c1984 as 360/12WB, meaning 'with binding' on body front edge, in contrast to 360/12 in Style Eleven, which has no binding on front body edge.

360/12BWB 1983–84 *Vintage reissue based on 1964-period original.*

360/12C63 2001–current *Vintage reissue based on 1963-period original. Renamed version of 360/12V64.*

360/12OS *See 360/12 listing.*

360/12V64 1984–2000 *Vintage reissue based on 1964-period original. Renamed 360/12C63 in 2001.*

360/12WB *See 360/12 listing, 370/12 listing.*

360/12WBBS *See 360/12 listing.*

365 1958–76, 1985–2007 *Trianglo markers, two pickups, vibrato tailpiece.*
Style nine
- Glued-in neck with bound fingerboard, triangle markers; 21 frets (24 frets phased in from c1969).
- Semi-acoustic bound body with one soundhole; sunburst, natural, or colours.
- Two pickups.
- Four controls (two volume, two tone; fifth 'blend' control added from c1963) and three-way selector, all on pickguard; side-mounted jack(s).
- Two-tier gold plastic pickguard

(white plastic from c1963).
- Six-saddle bridge, separate vibrato tailpiece.
Earliest examples with two controls (volume, tone) and one or two three-way selectors on single gold plastic pickguard.
SO (Special Order) examples available from 1964.
Available as 360WBVB (360 with vibrato tailpiece option, thus 365 specification) from 1985.

370 1958–2007 *Triangle markers, three pickups.*
Style nine
- Glued-in neck with bound fingerboard, triangle markers; 21 frets (24 frets phased in from c1969).
- Semi-acoustic bound body with one soundhole; sunburst, natural, or colours.
- Three pickups.
- Four controls (two volume, two tone; fifth 'blend' control added from c1963) and three-way selector, all on pickguard; side-mounted jack(s).
- Two-tier gold plastic pickguard (white plastic from c1963).
- Six-saddle bridge, separate tailpiece.
Earliest examples with two controls (volume, tone) and one or two three-

142

way selectors on single gold plastic pickguard.

SO (Special Order) examples available 1964–84.

Available as 370WB (meaning 'with binding' on body front edge, in contrast to 370 in Stylo Eleven, which has no binding on front body edge) or as 360WB with third-pickup option (thus 370 specification) from 1984.

370WB *See 370 listing.*

370WBVB *See 375 listing.*

370/12 1964–2007 *12 strings, triangle markers, three pickups.*
Style nine

■ Glued-in neck with bound fingerboard, triangle markers; 21 frets (24 frets phased in from c1969); 12-string headstock.
■ Semi-acoustic bound body with one soundhole; sunburst, natural, or colours.
■ Three pickups.
■ Five controls (two volume, two tone, one blend) and three-way selector, all on pickguard; side-mounted jacks.
■ Six-saddle bridge, separate tailpiece.

Known from 1964 as 370/12OS, meaning 'old style' body with front

binding, later changed to 370/12WBBS, meaning 'white binding both sides', until 1984.

Available as 370/12WB (meaning 'with binding' on body front edge, in contrast to 370 in Style Eleven, which has no binding on front body edge) or as 360/12WB with third-pickup option (thus 370/12WB specification) from 1984.

370/12OS *See 370/12 listing.*

370/12WB *See 370/12 listing.*

370/12WBBS *See 370/12 listing.*

375 1958–74, 1985–2007 *Triangle markers, three pickups, vibrato tailpiece.*
Style nine

■ Glued-in neck with bound fingerboard, triangle markers; 21 frets.
■ Semi-acoustic bound body with one soundhole; sunburst, natural, or colours.
■ Three pickups.
■ Four controls (two volume, two tone; fifth 'blend' control added from c1963) and three-way selector, all on pickguard; side-mounted jack(s).
■ Two-tier gold plastic pickguard (white plastic from c1963).

■ Six-saddle bridge, separate vibrato tailpiece.

Earliest examples with two controls (volume, tone) and one or two three-way selectors on single gold plastic pickguard.

SO (Special Order) examples available from 1964.

Available as 370WBVB (370 with vibrato tailpiece option, thus 375 specification) from 1985

381 first version 1958–63 *Hollow carved deep body, single gold plastic pickguard.*
Style nine

■ Glued-in neck with bound fingerboard, triangle markers; 21 frets.
■ Hollow, carved-top, back-bound body with one soundhole; sunburst or natural.
■ Two pickups.
■ Two controls (volume, tone) and two three-way selectors, all on pickguard; side-mounted jack(s).
■ Gold plastic pickguard.
■ Six-saddle bridge, separate tailpiece.
Some early examples with dot fingerboard markers.

381 second version 1969–74 *Hollow carved deep body, two-tier white plastic pickguard.*

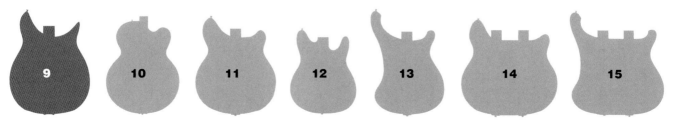

143

Style nine
- Glued-in neck with bound fingerboard, triangle markers; 21 frets.
- Hollow, carved-top, back-bound body with one soundhole; sunburst, natural, or colours.
- Two pickups.
- Five controls (two volume, two tone, one blend) and three-way selector, all on pickguard; side-mounted jack(s).
- Two-tier white plastic pickguard.
- Six-saddle bridge, separate tailpiece.

381/12 1969–74 *12 strings, hollow carved deep body, two-tier white plastic pickguard.*
As 381 second version, except:
- 12-string headstock.
Examples seen with three pickups.

381JK JOHN KAY 1988–96 *Signature on pickguard.*
Style nine
- Glued-in neck with bound fingerboard, triangle markers; 21 frets.
- Hollow, carved-top, back-bound body with one soundhole; black only.
- Two humbucker pickups.
- Five controls (three volume, one

tone, one four-way rotary selector), three-way selector, and phase mini-switch, all on pickguard; side-mounted jacks; active circuit.
- Two-tier silver plastic pickguard.
- Six-saddle bridge, separate tailpiece.
- John Kay signature, 'Limited Edition', and Steppenwolf logo on pickguard.
Limited edition of 250.

381V69 1987–current *Vintage reissue based on 1969-period original.*

381/12V69 1988–current *12 strings, hollow carved deep body.*
As 381V69, except:
- 12-string headstock.
- 12-saddle bridge.
Vintage reissue based on 1969-period original.
Examples seen with three pickups.

1993 *See 330/12 listing.*

1997 1987–2000 *Vintage reissue supposedly based on Model 1997, the 1964-period export version of the 335. But the absence of a vibrato tailpiece makes it a 330, which was not the equivalent of original UK Model 1997. See also 335 listing.*

1997SPC 1992–2000 *As 1997 (above) but with three pickups.*

1997VB 1987–2000 *Vintage reissue based on 1964-period export version of the 335, with 'correct' vibrato tailpiece.*

1998 *See 345 listing.*

1998PT PETE TOWNSHEND
1987–88 *'Pete Townshend' on pickguard.*
Style nine
- Glued-in neck; dot markers; 21 frets.
- Semi-acoustic body with one soundhole; sunburst only.
- Three pickups.
- Five controls (two volume, two tone, one blend) and three-way selector, all on pickguard; side-mounted jack.
- Two-tier white plastic pickguard.
- Six-saddle bridge, separate tailpiece.
- 'Pete Townshend Limited Edition' on pickguard.
Limited edition of 250.
Name refers to Model 1998, the 1964-period export version of the 345. But the absence of a vibrato tailpiece makes it a 340, which was not the equivalent of original UK Model 1998.

3262 *See 336/12 listing.*

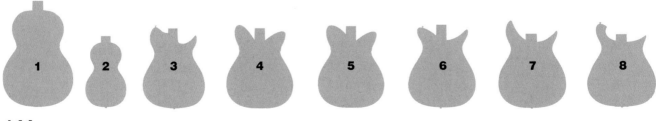

STYLE TEN

(1959–80)

Shallow right cutaway on large body

330F 1958–63 *Dot markers, two pickups.*

Style ten

- Glued-in neck; dot markers; 21 frets.
- Semi-acoustic body with one soundhole; sunburst or natural.
- Two pickups.
- Four controls (two volume, two tone; fifth 'blend' control added from c1963) and three-way selector, all on pickguard; side-mounted jack.
- Two-tier gold plastic pickguard (white plastic from c1963).
- Six-saddle bridge, separate tailpiece.

335F 1958–63 *Dot markers, two pickups, vibrato tailpiece.*

Style ten

- Glued-in neck; dot markers; 21 frets.
- Semi-acoustic body with one soundhole; sunburst or natural.
- Two pickups.
- Four controls (two volume, two tone; fifth 'blend' control added from c1963) and three-way selector, all on pickguard; side-mounted jack.
- Two-tier gold plastic pickguard (white plastic from c1963).
- Six-saddle bridge, separate vibrato.

340F 1958–63 *Dot markers, three pickups.*

Style ten

- Glued-in neck; dot markers; 21 frets
- Semi-acoustic body with one soundhole; sunburst or natural
- Three pickups.
- Four controls (two volume, two tone; fifth 'blend' control added from c1963) and three-way selector, all on pickguard; side-mounted jack.
- Two-tier gold plastic pickguard (white plastic from c1963).
- Six-saddle bridge, separate tailpiece.

345F 1958–63 *Dot markers, three pickups, vibrato tailpiece.*

Style ten

- Glued-in neck; dot markers; 21 frets.
- Semi-acoustic body with one soundhole; sunburst or natural.
- Three pickups.
- Four controls (two volume, two tone; fifth 'blend' control added from c1963) and three-way selector, all on pickguard; side-mounted jack.
- Two-tier gold plastic pickguard (white plastic from c1963).
- Six-saddle bridge, separate vibrato tailpiece.

360F first version 1958–63 *Triangle markers, two pickups, controls on pickguard.*

Style ten

- Glued-in neck with bound fingerboard, triangle markers; 21 frets.
- Semi-acoustic bound body with one soundhole; sunburst or natural.
- Two pickups.
- Four controls (two volume, two tone; fifth 'blend' control added from c1963) and three-way selector, all on pickguard; side-mounted jack(s).
- Two-tier gold plastic pickguard (white plastic from c1963).
- Six-saddle bridge, separate tailpiece.

360F second version 1966–70 *Triangle markers, two pickups, controls on body.*

Style ten

- Glued-in neck with bound fingerboard, triangle markers; 21 frets.
- Semi-acoustic bound body with one soundhole; sunburst or natural.
- Two pickups.
- Five controls (two volume, two tone, one blend) and three-way selector, all on body front; side-mounted jacks.
- White plastic pickguard.
- Six-saddle bridge, separate tailpiece.

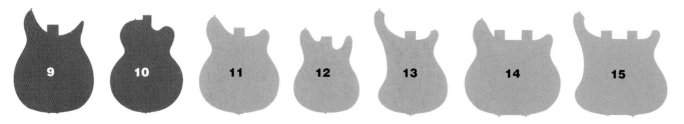

145

360/12F 1973–80 *12 strings, triangle markers, two pickups, controls on body.*

Style ten

- Glued-in neck with bound fingerboard, triangle markers; 21 frets; 12-string headstock.
- Semi-acoustic bound body with one soundhole; sunburst or natural.
- Two pickups.
- Five controls (two volume, two tone, one blend) and three-way selector, all on body front; side-mounted jacks.
- White plastic pickguard.
- Six-saddle bridge, separate tailpiece.

Some examples before 1973, built to special order.

365F first version 1958–63 *Triangle markers, two pickups, controls on pickguard, vibrato tailpiece.*

Style ten

- Glued-in neck with bound fingerboard, triangle markers; 21 frets.
- Semi-acoustic bound body with one soundhole; sunburst or natural.
- Two pickups.
- Four controls (two volume, two tone; fifth 'blend' control added from c1963) and three-way selector, all on pickguard; side-mounted jack(s).
- Two-tier gold plastic pickguard (white plastic from c1963).
- Six-saddle bridge, separate vibrato tailpiece.

365F second version 1966–70

Triangle markers, two pickups, controls on body, vibrato tailpiece.

Style ten

- Glued-in neck with bound fingerboard, triangle markers; 21 frets.
- Semi-acoustic bound body with one soundhole; sunburst or natural.
- Two pickups.
- Five controls (two volume, two tone, one blend) and three-way selector, all on body front; side-mounted jacks.
- White plastic pickguard.
- Six-saddle bridge, separate vibrato tailpiece.

370F first version 1958–63 *Triangle markers, three pickups, controls on pickguard.*

Style ten

- Glued-in neck with bound fingerboard, triangle markers; 21 frets.
- Semi-acoustic bound body with one soundhole; sunburst or natural.
- Three pickups.
- Four controls (two volume, two tone; fifth 'blend' control added from c1963) and three-way selector, all on pickguard; side-mounted jack(s).
- Two-tier gold plastic pickguard (white plastic from c1963).
- Six-saddle bridge, separate tailpiece.

370F second version 1966–70

Triangle markers, three pickups, controls on body.

Style ten

- Glued-in neck with bound fingerboard, triangle markers; 21 frets.
- Semi-acoustic bound body with one soundhole; sunburst or natural.
- Three pickups.
- Five controls (two volume, two tone, one blend) and three-way selector, all on body front; side-mounted jacks.
- White plastic pickguard.
- Six-saddle bridge, separate tailpiece.

375F first version 1958–63 *Triangle markers, three pickups, controls on body, vibrato tailpiece.*

Style ten

- Glued-in neck with bound fingerboard, triangle markers; 21 frets.
- Semi-acoustic bound body with one soundhole; sunburst or natural.

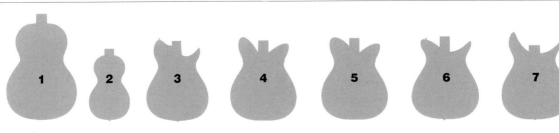

- Three pickups.
- Four controls (two volume, two tone; fifth 'blend' control added from c1963) and three-way selector, all on pickguard; side-mounted jack(s).
- Two-tier gold plastic pickguard (white plastic from c1963).
- Six-saddle bridge, separate vibrato tailpiece.

375F second version 1966-70
Triangle markers, three pickups, controls on body, vibrato tailpiece.
Style ten
- Glued-in neck with bound fingerboard, triangle markers; 21 frets.
- Semi-acoustic bound body with one soundhole; sunburst or natural.
- Three pickups.
- Five controls (two volume, two tone, one blend) and three-way selector, all on body front; side-mounted jacks.
- White plastic pickguard.
- Six-saddle bridge, separate vibrato tailpiece.

STYLE ELEVEN
(1964-current)
Offset cutaways (with rounded horns; 'sweeping crescent' profile across both cutaways) on large body – often known

as the 'rounded edge' style for deluxe big-body models

360 1964-current *Triangle markers, two pickups.*
Style eleven
- Glued-in neck with bound fingerboard, triangle markers; 21 frets (24 frets phased in from c1969).
- Semi-acoustic rear-edge-bound body with one bound soundhole; sunburst, natural, or colours.
- Two pickups.
- Five controls (two volume, two tone, one blend) and three-way selector, all on pickguard; side-mounted jacks.
- Two-tier white plastic pickguard.
- Six-saddle bridge, separate tailpiece.

360CW CARL WILSON 2000
Signature on pickguard.
Style eleven
- Glued-in neck with bound fingerboard, triangle markers; 21 frets.
- Semi-acoustic rear-edge-bound body with one bound soundhole; sunburst or black.
- Two pickups.
- Five controls (two volume, two tone, one blend) and three-way selector,

all on pickguard; side-mounted jacks.
- Two-tier white plastic pickguard.
- Six-saddle bridge, separate tailpiece.
- Carl Wilson signature, 'Limited Edition', and 'Made In America' logo on pickguard
Limited edition of 309, plus small number given to Wilson family.

360SPC TUXEDO 6 1987 *All-white, including fingerboard.*
Style eleven
As 360, except:
- White neck, fingerboard, and body.
- Two-tier black plastic pickguard.
- Black-plated hardware.

360VB *See 365 listing.*

360/12 1964-current *12 strings, triangle markers, two pickups.*
Style eleven
- Glued-in neck with bound fingerboard, triangle markers; 21 frets (24 frets phased in from c1969); 12-string headstock.
- Semi-acoustic rear-edge-bound body with one bound soundhole; sunburst, natural, or colours.
- Two pickups.
- Five controls (two volume, two tone, one blend) and three-way selector,

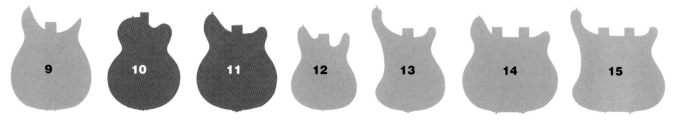

all on pickguard; side-mounted jacks.

■ Two-tier white plastic pickguard.

■ Six-saddle bridge, separate tailpiece.

360/12CW CARL WILSON 2000 *12 strings, signature on pickguard.*
As 360CW Carl Wilson, except:

■ 12-string headstock.

Limited edition of 186, including 2 left-hand examples, plus small number given to Wilson family.

360/12SPC TUXEDO 12 1987 *12 strings, all-white, including fingerboard.*
Style eleven
As 360/12, except:

■ White neck, fingerboard, and body.

■ Two-tier black plastic pickguard.

■ Black-plated hardware.

365 1964–76, 1985–2007 *Triangle markers, two pickups, vibrato tailpiece.*
Style eleven

■ Glued-in neck with bound fingerboard, triangle markers; 21 frets (24 frets phased in from c1969).

■ Semi-acoustic rear-edge-bound body with one bound soundhole; sunburst, natural, or colours.

■ Two pickups.

■ Five controls (two volume, two tone, one blend) and three-way selector, all on pickguard; side-mounted jack.

■ Two-tier white plastic pickguard.

■ Six-saddle bridge, separate vibrato tailpiece.

Available as 360VB (360 with vibrato tailpiece option, thus 365 specification) from 1985.

366/12 1966–76 *12 strings, triangle markers, two pickups, 12/6-string converter unit.*
As 360/12, except:

■ 12/6-string converter on body.

370 1964–2007 *Triangle markers, three pickups.*
Style eleven

■ Glued-in neck with bound fingerboard, triangle markers; 21 frets (24 frets phased in from c1969).

■ Semi-acoustic rear-edge-bound body with one bound soundhole; sunburst, natural, or colours.

■ Three pickups.

■ Five controls (two volume, two tone, one blend) and three-way selector, all on pickguard; side-mounted jacks.

■ Two-tier white plastic pickguard.

■ Six-saddle bridge, separate tailpiece.

Available as 360 with third-pickup option (thus 370 specification) 1986–90.

370VB *See 375 listing.*

370/12 1964–current *12 strings, triangle markers, three pickups.*
Style eleven

■ Glued-in neck with bound fingerboard, triangle markers; 21 frets (24 frets phased in from c1969); 12-string headstock.

■ Semi-acoustic rear-edge-bound body with one bound soundhole; sunburst, natural, or colours.

■ Three pickups.

■ Five controls (two volume, two tone, one blend) and three-way selector, all on pickguard; side-mounted jacks.

■ Two-tier white plastic pickguard.

■ Six-saddle bridge, separate tailpiece.

Available as 360/12 with third-pickup option (thus 370/12 specification) 1986–90.

370/12RM ROGER McGUINN *See 370/12RME1 listing.*

370/12RME1 ROGER McGUINN 1988–89 *12 strings, signature on pickguard.*
Style eleven

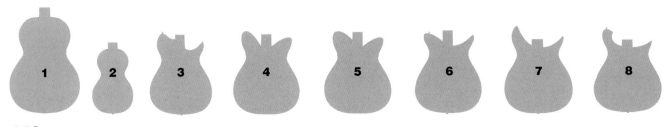

- Glued-in neck with bound fingerboard, triangle markers; 21 frets.
- Semi-acoustic rear edge-bound body with one bound soundhole; sunburst, natural, or black.
- Three pickups.
- Five controls (four volume, six-way rotary tone/compression selector) and three-way selector, all on pickguard; active circuit; side-mounted jacks.
- Two-tier white plastic pickguard.
- 12-saddle bridge, separate tailpiece.
- Roger McGuinn signature and 'Limited Edition' on pickguard.

Limited edition of 1,000.
Some examples without active circuit and with regular control layout, known as 370/12RM.

375 1964–75, 1985–2007 *Triangle markers, three pickups, vibrato tailpiece.*
Style eleven
- Glued-in neck with bound fingerboard, triangle markers; 21 frets (24 frets phased in from c1969).
- Semi-acoustic rear-edge-bound body with one bound soundhole; sunburst, natural, or colours.
- Three pickups.
- Five controls (two volume, two tone,

one blend) and three-way selector, all on pickguard; side-mounted jacks.
- Two-tier white plastic pickguard.
- Six-saddle bridge, separate vibrato tailpiece.

Available as 370VB (370 with vibrato tailpiece option, thus 375 specification), or 360 with third-pickup and vibrato-tailpiece options (thus 375 specification) from 1985.

380L LAGUNA 1996–2006 *No pickguard, gold hardware.*
Style eleven
- Glued-in neck with bound maple fingerboard, dot markers; 24 frets.
- Semi-acoustic rear-edge-bound body with one bound soundhole; walnut.
- Two pickups.
- Five controls (two volume, two tone, one blend) and three-way selector, all on body; side-mounted jacks.
- No pickguard.
- Six-saddle bridge/tailpiece.
- Gold-plated hardware.
Also 380LPZ Laguna with saddle-mounted piezo pickups.

380LPZ LAGUNA *See 380L Laguna listing.*

(1971–2001)
Offset cutaways with rounded horns on small body

220 HAMBURG 1992–96 *Maple fingerboard, two controls and selector, chrome hardware.*
Style twelve
- Bolt-on neck with maple fingerboard, dot markers; 25-inch scale, 24 frets.
- Solid body; sunburst, natural, or colours.
- Two pickups.
- Two controls (volume, tone) and three-way selector, all on pickguard; side-mounted jack.
- White plastic pickguard.
- Six-saddle bridge/tailpiece.

230GF GLENN FREY 1992–2001
Signature on pickguard.
Style twelve
- Bolt-on neck; dot markers; 25-inch scale, 24 frets.
- Contoured solid body; all-black only.
- Two pickups.
- Two controls (volume, tone) and three-way selector, all on pickguard; side-mounted jack.
- Silver plastic pickguard.
- Six-saddle bridge/tailpiece.
- Black-plated hardware.

■ Glenn Frey signature and 'Limited Edition' on pickguard.
Limited edition of 240, including 6 left-hand examples.

230 HAMBURG 1983–92 *Rosewood fingerboard, four controls and selector, chrome hardware.*
Style twelve
■ Bolt-on neck; dot markers; 25-inch scale, 24 frets.
■ Solid body; sunburst, natural, colours.
■ Two pickups.
■ Four controls (two volume, two tone) and three-way selector, all on body front; side-mounted jack.
■ Six-saddle bridge/tailpiece.

250 EL DORADO 1983–92 *Bound rosewood fingerboard, four controls and selector, gold hardware.*
Style twelve
■ Bolt-on neck with bound fingerboard, dot markers; 25-inch scale, 24 frets.
■ Solid bound body; sunburst, natural, or colours.
■ Two pickups.
■ Four controls (two volume, two tone) and three-way selector, all on body front; side-mounted jack.
■ Six-saddle bridge/tailpiece.
■ Gold-plated hardware.

260 EL DORADO 1992–96 *Maple fingerboard, two controls and selector, gold hardware.*
Style twelve
■ Bolt-on neck with maple fingerboard, dot markers; 25-inch scale, 24 frets.
■ Solid bound body; sunburst, natural, or colours.
■ Two pickups.
■ Two controls (volume, tone) and three-way selector, all on pickguard; side-mounted jack.
■ Chrome-plated metal pickguard.
■ Six-saddle bridge/tailpiece.
■ Gold-plated hardware.

430 1971–82 *Rosewood fingerboard, four controls and selector, black plastic pickguard.*
Style twelve
■ Bolt-on neck; dot markers; 25-inch scale, 24 frets.
■ Solid body; sunburst, natural, colours.
■ Two pickups.
■ Four controls (two volume, two tone), three-way selector, and jack, all on pickguard.
■ Black plastic pickguard.
■ Six-saddle bridge/tailpiece.

(1973–83)
Offset cutaways (with hooked long left horn; 'high cresting wave' profile across both cutaways) on small body

480 1973–83 *Two pickups.*
Style thirteen
■ Bolt-on neck with bound fingerboard, dot markers; 25-inch scale, 24 frets.
■ Solid body; sunburst, natural, or colours.
■ Two pickups.
■ Four controls (two volume, two tone) and three-way selector, all on pickguard; side-mounted jack.
■ White plastic pickguard.
■ Six-saddle bridge, separate tailpiece.

481 1974–83 *Slanted frets, pickups, and bridge.*
Style thirteen
■ Bolt-on neck with bound fingerboard, triangle markers; 25-inch scale, 24 slanted frets.
■ Solid bound body; sunburst, natural, or colours.
■ Two slanted pickups.
■ Four controls (two volume, two tone), three-way selector, and phase mini-switch, all on pickguard; side-mounted jack.

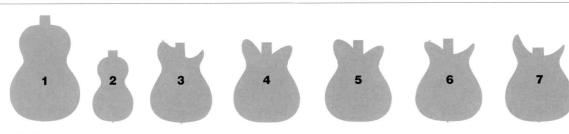

- White plastic pickguard.
- Six-saddle slanted bridge, separate tailpiece.

483 1980–83 *Three pickups.*
Style thirteen
- Bolt-on neck with bound fingerboard, dot markers; 25 inch scale, 24 frets.
- Solid body; sunburst, natural, or colours.
- Three pickups.
- Four controls (two volume, two tone) and three-way selector, all on pickguard; side-mounted jack.
- White plastic pickguard.
- Six-saddle bridge, separate tailpiece.

STYLE FOURTEEN
(1975–92)
Offset cutaways with rounded horns on double-neck large body

362/12 1975–92 *12-string and 6-string necks.*
Style fourteen
- Glued-in necks with bound fingerboards, triangle markers; 24 frets per neck.
- Semi-acoustic bound body with one bound soundhole; sunburst, natural, or colours.

- Two pickups per neck.
- Five controls (two volume, two tone, one blend) and two three-way selectors, all on pickguard; side-mounted jacks.
- White plastic pickguard.
- Six-saddle bridge, separate tailpiece per neck.

STYLE FIFTEEN
(1975–92)
Offset cutaways with hooked long left horn on double-neck large body

4080 1975–92 *Four-string bass and six-string guitar necks.*
Style fifteen
- Bolt-on necks with bound fingerboards, triangle markers; 20 frets on bass neck, 24 frets on guitar neck.
- Solid bound body; sunburst, natural, or colours.
- Two pickups per neck.
- Five controls (two volume, two tone, one blend) and two three-way selectors, all on pickguard; side-mounted jacks.
- Black plastic pickguard.
- Four-saddle bridge/tailpiece for bass neck; six-saddle bridge, separate tailpiece for guitar neck.

4080/12 1977–92 *Four-string bass and twelve-string guitar necks.*
Style fifteen
- Bolt-on necks with bound fingerboards, triangle markers; 20 frets on bass neck, 24 frets on 12-string neck.
- Solid bound body; sunburst, natural, or colours.
- Two pickups per neck.
- Five controls (two volume, two tone, one blend) and two three-way selectors, all on pickguard; side-mounted jacks.
- Black plastic pickguard.
- Four-saddle bridge/tailpiece for bass neck; six-saddle bridge, separate tailpiece for 12-string neck.

9   10   11   12   13   14   15

MISCELLANEOUS MAKES AND MODELS

Rickenbacker manufactured some guitars that did not carry the usual brand.

ASTRO AS-51 (1964)
Unique-shape solid body; offset dot markers and one pickup; marketed as a 'kit of parts' guitar.

CONTELLO 425 (1962)
Based on Rickenbacker 425 with Style 8 body shape, but with Contello logo on headstock.

ELECTRO ES-16 (1964–71)
Based on Rickenbacker Model 1000 with Style 6 body shape, but pickup located midway between neck and bridge. Electro logo on headstock. Sold as part of a set with companion amplifier.

ELECTRO ES-17 (1964–75)
Based on Rickenbacker 425 with Style 8 body shape, but pickup located midway between neck and bridge. Electro logo on headstock. Sold as part of a set with companion amplifier.

RYDER 425 (1963) *Based on Rickenbacker 425 with Style 8 body shape, but with Ryder logo on headstock.*

DATING RICKENBACKER GUITARS

Finding the age of an instrument is a priority for most owners. This can be satisfying for its own sake, but often age can have a direct bearing on value, particularly for examples deemed to be 'vintage'. The Rickenbacker company has been responsible for a selection of models that have since become collectables, and as always an association with famous names is the most influential factor.

Some Rickenbackers are difficult to date with scientific precision, and an approximate age should be considered a safe ideal. Serial numbers can help, although they don't always provide an exact year.

The system employed by Rickenbacker since 1960 is generally regarded to be more accurate than most, suggesting that the company applied the numbers with more diligence and consistency than many contemporary makers. This is fortunate, because a number of models, such as the vintage reissues, do look very similar, and the serial number must then play a role in identifying the true production period.

Prior to 1960, things were not so straightforward. Many 30s and 40s models did not come with serial numbers, so there is no help for dating there. Into the 50s, and the situation improves a little. The assorted Combos and Models had serial numbers between five and seven characters long. Of these, the first, second, or third was a letter, and the digit following this letter denotes the production year, indicating the last digit of 195X.

For example:
6C7161. The 7, following the C, indicates 1957.
V98. The 9, following the V, indicates 1959.

Unfortunately this method was not used consistently, and there are certainly exceptions. It was not used for the semi-acoustic models of the same period, which have serial numbers with little coherence and, thus, no relevance to dating.

In late 1960, Rickenbacker began a new system applied with apparently logical consistency for the next 26 years. This revised scheme has a two-letter coded prefix followed by a two, three, or four-digit number. The first letter indicates the year and the second the month. The tables following have complete lists that will help you translate these codes.

First letter in prefix = year

A – 1961
B – 1962
C – 1963
D – 1964
E – 1965
F – 1966
G – 1967
H – 1968
I – 1969
J – 1970
K – 1971
L – 1972
M – 1973
N – 1974
O – 1975
P – 1976
Q – 1977
R – 1978
S – 1979
T – 1980
U – 1981
V – 1982
W – 1983
X – 1984
Y – 1985
Z – 1986

Second letter in prefix = month

A   January
B – February
C – March
D – April
E – May
F – June
G – July
H – August
I – September
J – October
K – November
L – December
M – January
N – February
O – March
P – April
Q – May
R – June
S – July
T – August
U – September
V – October
W – November
X – December

For example:
DB 123. The D indicates 1964; the B indicates February.
XJ 1375. The X indicates 1984; the J indicates October.

Rickenbacker last used the two-letter system in 1986 and then started a new system, beginning the following year and again using a coded format. The two-character prefix was now a letter and a digit, followed again by a two, three, or four-digit number. The letter in the prefix still indicates the month, with the same translations, while the prefix digit indicates the year. The table below has a list that should help you translate these year codes.

Digit after letter in prefix = year
0 – 1987
1 – 1988
2 – 1989
3 – 1990
4 – 1991
5 – 1992
6 – 1993
7 – 1994
8 – 1995
9 – 1996
0 – 1997
1 – 1998

For example:
H5 5944. The 5 in the prefix indicates 1992.
C8 9024. The 8 in the prefix indicates 1995.

Rickenbacker last used that system in 1998 and from that year adopted an easier style of numbering. Now the first two digits indicate the last two digits of the year, followed by a five-digit serial. The table shows how this works so far.

Two-digit prefix = year
98 – 1998
99 – 1999
00 – 2000
01 – 2001
02 – 2002
03 – 2003
04 – 2004
05 – 2005
06 – 2006
07 – 2007
08 – 2008
09 – 2009
10 – 2010

For example:
00 25882. The 00 prefix indicates 2000.
09 30485. The 09 prefix indicates 2009.

Rickenbacker serial numbers are stamped on the bridge, neckplate, or (most commonly) the jackplate. The fact that the jackplate is easily removable means that exchanging one for a more valuable (usually earlier) example is easy. For that reason, if you use the serial number to date a guitar it's best to try to match it with other dating clues. Rickenbacker did make some overall changes to components and cosmetics, mainly in the mid 60s, which can serve as useful pointers when you're trying to find the age of some instruments. We'll discuss some of these to close this section.

Rickenbacker made a distinctive modification between 1961 and 1963, adding a **fifth control** to the regular two-volume/two-tone layout. This fifth control had a smaller knob and was designed to blend tones. The **Rick-O-Sound** pseudo-stereo system, introduced as a standard feature on deluxe models from 1960, has a jackplate with two output jacks. Around 1963, Rickenbacker changed the **pickguard** and **truss-rod cover** to white plastic,

153

replacing the gold-coloured plastic used on earlier instruments. The original flat 'trapeze' **tailpiece** was replaced on most models during 1963 by one in the shape of a large 'R'.

The 300 family of models shifted from 21 frets to **24 frets** about 1969. **Hi-Gain pickups**, with black tops, were introduced around 1969. The triangle markers of deluxe models became **less wide** about 1970.

The metal casing of some American-made control potentiometers (usually called **pots**) are stamped with code numbers that, when translated, can provide a useful confirmation of the instrument's approximate age – although bear in mind that the pots may have been changed since the guitar was made. Pots have a number of six or seven digits. The first three identify the manufacturer and can be ignored. The next one or two digits show the year: one shows the last digit of 195X; a pair indicates any year after the 50s. The final two digits signify the week of the appropriate year.

MODEL CHRONOLOGY

This listing shows all the models that were produced by Rickenbacker in the chronological order of their introduction. The number on the left refers to our 'body Style' or shape.

1	**Electro Spanish**	1932–35
2	**Electro Spanish**	1935–42
1	**Ken Roberts**	1935–40
2	**Vibrola Spanish** 1937–42	
1	**S-59**	1940–42
1	**Spanish**	1946–50
3	**Combo 600**	1954–59
3	**Combo 800**	1954–59
4	**Combo 400**	1956–57
6	**Combo 400**	1957–58
4	**Combo 450**	1957
6	**Combo 450**	1957–58
7	**Combo 650**	1957–59
7	**Combo 850**	1957–59
5	**Combo 900**	1957
5	**Combo 950**	1957
6	**Model 900**	1957–71
6	**Model 950**	1957–71
4	**Model 1000**	1957
6	**Model 1000**	1957–71
7	**310**	1958–71, 1981–84

7	**315**	1958–75
7	**320**	1958–92
7	**325**	1958–75, 1985–92
9	**330**	1958–current
10	**330F**	1958–63
9	**335**	1958–77, 1985–2007
10	**335F**	1958–63
9	**340**	1958–2007
10	**340F**	1958–63
9	**345**	1958–75, 1985–2007
10	**345F**	1958–63
9	**360**	1958–1995
10	**360F**	1958–63, 1966–70
9	**365**	1958–76, 1985–2007
10	**365F**	1958–63, 1966–70
9	**370**	1958–2007
10	**370F**	1958–63, 1966–70
9	**375**	1958–74, 1985–2007
10	**375F**	1958–63, 1966–70
9	**381**	1958–63, 1969–74
8	**425**	1958–72
8	**450**	1958–85
8	**460**	1961–85
8	**615**	1962–74, 1985
8	**625**	1962–74, 1985
11	**360**	1964–current
9	**360/12**	1964–95
11	**360/12**	1964–current
11	**365**	1964–76, 1985–2007
11	**370**	1964–2007
9	**370/12**	1964–2007
11	**370/12**	1964–current
11	**375**	1964–75, 1985–2007
8	**450/12**	1964–85
9	**330/12**	1965–current
8	**420**	1965–83

9	**336/12**	1966–76
11	**366/12**	1966–76
8	**456/12**	1966–75
9	**381/12**	1969–74
9	**331**	1970–76
9	**331/12**	1970–75
12	**430**	1971–82
8	**900**	1971–79
8	**950**	1971–79
10	**360/12F**	1973–80
13	**480**	1973–83
13	**481**	1974–83
8	**620**	1974–current
14	**362/12**	1975–92
15	**4080**	1975–92
15	**4080/12**	1977–92
9	**340/12**	1980–2007
13	**483**	1980–83
8	**620/12**	1981–current
12	**230 Hamburg**	1983–92
12	**250 El Dorado**	1983–92
7	**320B**	1983–84
7	**325B**	1983–84
7	**350 Liverpool**	1983–95
7	**355 Liverpool Plus** 1983–85	
9	**360/12BWB**	1983–84
7	**325V59**	1984–2000
7	**325V63**	1984–2000

9 **360/12V64** 1984–2000

7 **325/12** 1985–86

8 **610** 1985–95

11 **360PC Tuxedo 6** 1987

11 **360/12SPC Tuxedo 12**
   1987

9 **381V69** 1987–current

9 **1997** 1987–2000

9 **1997VB** 1987–2000

9 **1998PT Pete**
   Townshend 1987–88

7 **350SH Susanna Hoffs**
   1988–90

11 **370/12RME1 Roger**
   McGuinn 1988–89

9 **381JK John Kay**
   1988–96

9 **381/12V69** 1988–current

8 **610/12** 1988–95

7 **325JL John Lennon**
   1989–93

7 **355JL John Lennon**
   1989–93

7 **355JLVB John Lennon**
   1989–93

7 **355/12JL John Lennon**
   1989–93

9 **360V64** 1991–current

8 **660/12TP Tom Petty**
   1991–96

8 **650E Excalibur** 1991–95

12 **220 Hamburg** 1992–96

12 **230GF Glenn Frey**
   1992–2001

12 **260 El Dorado** 1992–96

8 **650A Atlantis**
   1992–2002

9 **1997SPC** 1992–2000

8 **650C Colorado**
   1993–current

8 **650D Dakota** 1993–2007

8 **650S Sierra** 1993–2007

7 **350V63** 1994–current

7 **350/12V63** 1994–2007

8 **650F Frisco** 1995–2002

11 **380L Laguna** 1996–2006

8 **660** 1999 current

8 **660/12** 1999–current

11 **360CW Carl Wilson**
   2000

11 **360/12CW Carl Wilson**
   2000

7 **325C58 Hamburg**
   2001–08

7 **325C64 Miami**
   2001–current

9 **360/12C63** 2001–current

7 **1996** 2007

Index

Page numbers in *italics* indicate illustrations. Page numbers from 130 to 151 indicate entries in the model directory at the back of the book. Song titles etc whose first word is a 'The' or 'A' are listed under the second word of the title; for example 'The Waiting' is under W.

157

Acknowledgements

INSTRUMENT OWNERS
The guitars we photographed came from the collections of the following individuals and organisations, and we're grateful for their help. They are listed here in the alphabetical order of the code used to identify their instruments in the Key below. **AB** Andy Babiuk; **AM** Albert Molinaro; **DB** Dave Brewis; **DG** Dave Gregory; **EX** Experience Music Project; **GG** Graham Griffiths; **GH** George Harrison; **JN** John Nelson; **JS** John Sheridan; **JW** John Williams; **KC** Keith Clark; **MC** Mike Campbell; **MK** Martin Kelly; **MW** Michael Wright; **PD** Paul Day; **PQ** Pat Quilter; **RG** Robin Guthrie; **RI** Rickenbacker International Corporation; **SJ** Scott Jennings; **YO** Yoko Ono.

KEY TO INSTRUMENT PHOTOGRAPHS
The following key is designed to identify who owned which guitars at the time they were photographed. After the relevant bold-type page number(s) we list the model name followed by the owner's initials (see Instrument Owners above). **11** Frying Pan RI. **14–15** Electro Spanish wood GG; Electro Spanish Bakelite PQ; Roberts GG. **18–19** Spanish RI. **22–23** Combo 800 JN; Combo 400 KC. **26–27** Model 1000 SJ. **27** Combo 850 RI. **30–31** 360 SJ; 330 RI; 365 GG. **34–35** 375F RI. **35** 325 YO. **42–43** Twin PD; 460 AM. **46–47** Bellzouki MW; prototype JW. **47** Arden 360/12 SJ. **50–51** 360/12 GH. **54–55** Double Six PD. **58–59** 320/12 YO. **59** 450/12 SJ. **62** 1993 (trapeze) GG. **62–63** 1993 (R) MK. **63** 360/12 AB. **70–71** 370/12 (No.2) SJ; 360/12 (No.1) EX. **74–75** Electric XII RG. **75** Riviera DB. **79** Gretsch JS. **82–83** 456/12 RI; 366/12 GG. **83** 331 RI. **86–87** 360/12F GG. **87** 381/12V69 RI. **90–91** 481 RI. **94–95** 360/12 DG; 4080/12 RI; 362/12 GG. **95** 330 GG. **98–99** 360/12V64 RI. **99** 250 El Dorado RI. **102-103** 370/12RM RI. **103** 370/12RM firegло GG; 370/12RM jetglo GG. **110** 1998PT RI.

111 355/12JL RI; 381JK RI. **114–115** 660/12TP RI; 620/12 MC. **122–123** 360/12CW GG. **123** 360DCM (pickguard only) GG.

Principal guitar photography is by Nigel Bradley and Miki Slingsby. Other guitar pictures by Jeff Amberg (prototype p46–47); Garth Blore (Stratosphere p42–43; Double Six p54–55); Matthew Chattle (Riviera p75); Rick Gould/In Concert Photography (620/12 p114–115); Pat Graham (660/12 & 360 p98); Paul Kelly (1993 R p62–63); and Jeff Veitch (Arden 360/12 p47; 370/12 No.2 p70–71).

ARTIST PICTURES Bold-type page number, subject, and photographer/agency. **2** Harrison, David Redfern/Redferns. **35** Lennon, Evening Standard/Getty Images. **43** Leadbelly, Hulton Archive/Getty Images; Seeger, Gai Terrell/Redferns. **50** Lennon, David Magnus/Rex Features. **51** Beatles, Tony Gale/Pictorial Press. **55** Beatles, Max Scheler/K&K/Redferns. **59** Harrison, Bill Orchard/Rex Features. **70** McGuinn, Michael Ochs Archives/Getty Images. **71** McGuinn, Sony BMG Music Entertainment/Getty Images; Townshend, Colin Jones; Pender, Mike Prendergast. **74** Alpert (studio) Everett Collection/Rex Features. **75** Wilson, Chris Walter/Photofeatures. **79** Count Five, GAB Archive/Redferns; Turtles, Michael Ochs Archives/Getty Images. **87** Kantner, Robert Altman/Michael Ochs Archives/Getty Images. **90** Buckley, Ian Dickson/Redferns. **91** Rutherford, David Warner Ellis/Redferns; McLaughlin Chris Walter/Photofeatures; Page, Chris Walter/Photofeatures. **98** Buck/Marr, Pat Graham/Retna. **99** Willson-Piper, Anthony Collins (fee donated to Doug Flutie Jr. Foundation for Autism, www.flutiefoundation.org). **115** Petty, Brian Hineline/Retna; Campbell, Ebet Roberts/Redferns. **122** Cline, Dove Shore/Getty Images; Marr, Peter Doherty/Retna. **123** O'Brien, Shirlaine Forrest/WireImage/Getty Images.

MEMORABILIA illustrated in the book – advertisements, catalogues, patents, photographs, and so on – comes from the collections of Tony Bacon, Balafon Image Bank, Paul Day, Martin Kelly, The Music Trades, The National Jazz Archive (Loughton), John Pisano, Rickenbacker International Corporation, Alan Rogan, and vintaxe.com.

ORIGINAL INTERVIEWS for this book were conducted by Tony Bacon as follows: Suzi Arden (March 1994); Jim Babjak (July 2009); Andre Barreau (July 2009); Peter Buck (July 2009); Dick Burke (November 1993, April 1994); Mike Campbell (July 2009); Nels Cline (July 2009); Derek Davis (April 1994); Deke Dickerson (June 2009); Vic Flick (August 2009); Jeffrey Foskett (August 2009); Dave Gregory (July 2009); Robin Guthrie (July 2009); F.C. Hall (November 1993); John Hall (November 1993, April 1994; September 2009); Tony Hatch (July 2009); Chris Huston (March 1994); Paul Kantner (September 2009); Johnny Marr (August 2009); Mike Maxfield (July 2009); Ted McCarty (October 1992); Roger McGuinn (April 1994); Mike Pender (July 2009); Tom Petty (August 2009); John Pisano (June 2009); Tony Poole (June 2009); Don Randall (February 1992); Joe Talbot (August 1994); and Marty Willson-Piper (July 2009). All quotes from Rickenbacker documents, letters, and so on come from items in the RIC archive.

THANKS to the following people for help with this book (and the previous Bacon & Day work The Rickenbacker Book), in addition to those already named above: Roger Askey; Andy Babiuk; Alf Bicknell; Chris Bilheimer; Johnny Black; John Blaney; Julie Bowie; Dave Brewis (Stars Guitars); Steve Brown (vintaxe.com); Emma Busk (The Publicity Connection); Walter Carter; Lloyd Chiate (Voltage); Jim Cooper; Stephen Davidson; Jane, Sarah, and Simon Day; Deke Dickerson; André Duchossoir; Bertis Downs (R.E.M.); John Einarson; Ray Ennis; Ben Folsom (Curly R); Michael Gaiman; Linda Garson; Bill George; Barry Gibson (Burns London); Nick Hall (The Observer); Neil Harpe (stellaguitars.com); Tiare Helberg; Christopher Hjort; Larry Henrickson (Ax-In-Hand); Kate Herd (Music Sales); Tony Hoffman (Shadsfax); Steve Jolly (Holiday Music); Martin Kelly; Mary Klauzer (East End Management); Helmuth Lemme; Spencer Leigh; Jon Lewin; Peter Lewry; Dave Liddle; Lydia Lisle; Joel McIver; Karla Merrifeld; Gurf Morlix; Mark Mumford (Hal Leonard); Kevin O'Neil (R.E.M.); Greg Prevost; Ian Purser; Mark Radcliffe (BBC Radio 2); Heinz Rebellius; Julian Ridgway (Redferns); Alan Rogan; Emily Rosenblum (Tony Margherita Management); Martin Scott; Peter S. Shukat; Melinda Simms (Experience Music Project); Jeff Simpson (BBC Radio 1); Maggie Skinner (Experience Music Project); Kate Smith (Handmade Films); Trevor Smith; Steve Soest (Soest Guitar Repair); Toshio Sogabe (Rick's International Corp, Japan); George Tomsco; Kelly Wong (Retna).

SPECIAL THANKS to John Hall at Rickenbacker International Corporation for his generous hospitality, for allowing us to rummage freely through his (abundant) filing cabinets, and for letting us dismantle, strum, and photograph the guitar archive. To Graham Griffiths for allowing us access to his remarkable collection, which is strongly featured in this book. Also to Scott Jennings for lining up some wonderful instruments and for sharing his rich knowledge of Rickenbackers and Rickenbacker people with us. And to Paul Day, for his contributions to the vintage The Rickenbacker Book and its original reference section.

BOOKS

Andy Babiuk Beatles Gear: All The Fab Four's Instruments From Stage To Studio (Backbeat 2002).
Tony Bacon The Fender Electric Guitar Book: A Complete History Of Fender Instruments (Backbeat 2007); 50 Years Of Gretsch Electrics (Backbeat 2005); The History Of The American Guitar (Balafon/Friedman Fairfax 2001).
Tony Bacon (ed) Echo & Twang (Backbeat 2001); Feedback & Fuzz (Miller Freeman 2000); Electric Guitars: The Illustrated Encyclopedia (Thunder Bay 2000).
Tony Bacon & Paul Day The Rickenbacker Book (Balafon/Miller Freeman 1994); The Ultimate Guitar Book (DK/Knopf 1991).

Harry Benson The Beatles In The Beginning (Mainstream 1993).
Bob Brozman The History & Artistry Of National Resonator Instruments (Centerstream 1993).
Walter Carter The Gibson Electric Guitar Book: Seventy Years Of classic Guitars (Backbeat 2007).
Paul Day The Burns Book (PP 1979).
Geoff Emerick with Howard Massey Here, There And Everywhere (Gotham 2006).
Per Gjörde Pearls And Crazy Diamonds: Fifty Years Of Burns Guitars (Addot 2001)
George Gruhn & Walter Carter Gruhn's Guide To Vintage Guitars: An Identification Guide For American Fretted Instruments (Miller Freeman 1999).
Christopher Hjort So You Want to Be A Rock'n'Roll Star: The Byrds Day-By-Day 1965–73 (Jawbone 2008).
Steve Howe & Tony Bacon The Steve Howe Guitar Collection (Balafon/Miller Freeman 1994).
Mark Lewisohn The Complete Beatles Recording Sessions (Hamlyn 1988), The Complete Beatles Chronicle (Pyramid 1992).
Naoki Ogane Rickenbacker: Pioneer Of The Electric Guitar (Rittor 1995).
Mike Read, Nigel Goodall, Peter Lewry Cliff Richard: The Complete Chronicle (Hamlyn 1993).
Johnny Rogan Timeless Flight (Square One 1990).
Norbert Schnepel & Helmuth Lemme Elektro-Gitarren Made In Germany English translation JP Klink (Musik-Verlag Schnepel-Lemme 1988).
Richard Smith The Complete History Of Rickenbacker Guitars (Centerstream 1987).
Doug Tulloch Neptune Bound: The Ultimate Danelectro Gear Guide (Centerstream 2008).
Tom Wheeler American Guitars (HarperPerennial 1990).

BACK ISSUES We consulted old copies of the following magazines: Beat Instrumental; Beat Monthly; Billboard; Guitar Digest; The Guitar Magazine; Guitar Player; Guitar World; Guitarist; Making Music; The Music Trades; Observer Sunday Magazine; One Two Testing; 20th Century Guitar; Vintage Gallery; Vintage Guitar.

WEBSITES Useful sites included: danacountryman.com/vinnie/main.htm, geocities.com/vintage325, jackiedeshannon.tripod.com, rickbeat.com, rickenbacker.com, rickenbacker.me.uk, and rickresource.com (especially rickresource.com/register/index.php). Forums and message boards at websites can offer nuggets of good info among the unsubstantiated speculation. Those we looked at included billystrangemusic.ning.com, rickresource.com, rickenbacker.com, shadowmusic.tgis.co.uk, and 12stringguitarist.ning.com.

TRADEMARKS Throughout this book we have mentioned a number of registered trademark names. Rather than put the symbol for 'trademark' or 'registered' next to every occurrence of a trademarked name, we state here that we are using the names only in an editorial fashion and that we do not intend to infringe any trademarks.

UPDATES? The author and publisher welcome any new information for future editions. You can email us at ricktwelve@jawbonepress.com
or you can write to
Rickenbacker Electric 12-String, Backbeat UK, 2A Union Court, 20-22 Union Road, London SW4 6JP, England.

"I can feel a strange sensation taking place / I can hear the guitars playing lovely tunes."
'When You Walk In The Room' by Jackie DeShannon